DEL IVAN JANIK

The Curve of Return:
D. H. Lawrence's
Travel Books

EL S
EDITIONS

ELS Editions
Department of English
University of Victoria
Victoria, BC
Canada V8W 3W1
www.elseditions.com

Founding Editor: Samuel L. Macey

General Editor: Luke Carson

Printed by CreateSpace

English literary studies monograph series
ISSN 0829-7681 ; 22
ISBN-10 0-920604-42-0
ISBN-13 978-0-920604-42-7

CONTENTS

ACKNOWLEDGEMENTS

Barnes and Noble: *D. H. Lawrence: The Critical Heritage,* ed. R. P. Draper; *D. H. Lawrence: A Personal Record* by Jessie Chambers, ed. L. D. Chambers; *With D. H. Lawrence in New Mexico* by Knud Merrild.

Black Sparrow Press: *The Escaped Cock* by D. H. Lawrence, ed. Gerald M. Lacy.

University of California Press: *Poste Restante: A Lawrence Travel Calendar* by Harry T. Moore, Introduction by Mark Schorer.

The Press of Case Western Reserve University: *D. H. Lawrence's American Journey* by James C. Cowan.

University of Chicago Press: *The Utopian Vision of D. H. Lawrence* by Eugene Goodheart.

Columbia University Press: *D. H. Lawrence and Susan His Cow* by William York Tindall; *The Nature Novel from Hardy to Lawrence* by John Alcorn.

Faber and Faber: *The Forked Flame* by H. M. Daleski.

Farrar, Straus and Giroux: *The Priest of Love* by Harry T. Moore; *The World We Imagine* by Mark Schorer.

Grove Press: *Lady Chatterley's Lover* by D. H. Lawrence.

Heinemann: *Mornings in Mexico and Etruscan Places* by D. H. Lawrence.

Alfred A. Knopf: *The Plumed Serpent* by D. H. Lawrence.

McGill-Queens University Press: *The Quest for Rananim,* ed. George Zytaryuk.

Northwestern University Press: *The Visual Imagination of D. H. Lawrence* by Keith Aldritt.

University of Oklahoma Press: *The Achievement of D. H. Lawrence,* ed. Frederick J. Hoffman and Harry T. Moore.

Oxford University Press: *D. H. Lawrence and the New World* by David Cavitch; *Movements in European History* by D. H. Lawrence, ed. James Boulton.

University of South Carolina Press: *Another Ego* by Baruch Hochman.

Southern Illinois University Press: *D. H. Lawrence and the Dial* by Nicholas Joost and Alvin Sullivan; *D. H. Lawrence: The Man and His Work* by Émile Delavenay.

University of Texas Press: *Dark Night of the Body* by L. D. Clark.

Twayne: *D. H. Lawrence* by Ronald P. Draper.

Viking Press: *D. H. Lawrence and Italy,* Introduction by Anthony Burgess; *D. H. Lawrence; The World of the Five Major Novels* by Scott Sanders; *The Collected Letters of D. H. Lawrence,* ed. Harry T. Moore; *The Complete Poems of D. H. Lawrence,* ed. Vivian de Sola Pinto and F. Warren Roberts; *The Complete Short Stories of D. H. Lawrence; Psychoanalysis and the Unconscious and Fantasia of the Unconscious,* Introduction by Philip Rieff; *Phoenix,* ed. Edward McDonald; *Phoenix II,* ed. Warren Roberts and Harry T. Moore; *Aaron's Rod, Apocalypse, Etruscan Places, John Thomas and Lady Jane, Kangaroo, The Rainbow, Sea and Sardinia, Sons and Lovers, Studies in Classic American Literature, Twilight in Italy,* and *Women in Love* by D. H. Lawrence.

Yale University Press: *Toward Women in Love* by Stephen J. Miko.

NOTE ON THE TEXTS

All page references to Lawrence's travel books appear parenthetically in the text. For *Twilight in Italy* (TI), *Sea and Sardinia* (SS), and *Etruscan Places* (EP) the first citation refers to the first edition, the second to the Heinemann Phoenix edition, and the third to the Viking Compass edition. In the case of *Mornings in Mexico* (MM), the first reference is to the first edition, the second to the Heinemann Phoenix edition. Full publication information appears in the Bibliography.

PREFACE

D. H. Lawrence was a writer; although his primary reputation is, of course, as a novelist, he was a creditable writer in almost every genre and a distinguished artist in several. This is a fact that has only recently begun to be reflected in the subjects of critical books on his works. David J. Gordon's *D. H. Lawrence as a Literary Critic* (1966) was the first full-length study of Lawrence to focus specifically on his non-fiction prose. Tom Marshall's *The Psychic Mariner: A Reading of the Poems of D. H. Lawrence* appeared in 1970, and it has been followed by Sandra M. Gilbert's *Acts of Attention: The Poems of D. H. Lawrence* (1972) and *The Hostile Sun* (1973), a small but stimulating volume on the same subject by Joyce Carol Oates. More recently, Sylvia Sklar published *The Plays of D. H. Lawrence* (1975).

Lawrence's travel books, however, have continued to be slighted by serious students of literature. Eliot Fay's *Lorenzo in Search of the Sun: D. H. Lawrence in Italy, Mexico, and the American South-West* (1955) deals with the period of Lawrence's life during which he wrote his last three travel books, but in spite of his provocative title Fay uses them only as sources of biographical information. Passages from the travel books are occasionally cited in discussions of Lawrence's fiction to support interpretations of particular novels or stories or to illustrate aspects of his "metaphysic," but critics have rarely dealt at length with the travel books themselves, and they have not recognized the pattern in Lawrence's development as a thinker and artist that they implicitly trace. Yet Lawrence's four travel books are uniquely significant to an understanding of the writer and the man, because they seem to have provided a focus, at crucial points in his career, for his analysis of modern society and his search for a constructive and meaningful mode of living.

That search was, in the broadest sense of the term, religious. Like the early nineteenth-century Romantics, Lawrence rejected traditional religious doctrines but was unable to embrace the concept of a purely materialistic universe. Like them he sought spiritual meaning in life by pursuing the supernatural through the natural, unity through diversity. His travel books are, among other things, a record of that search and of his attempts to express its personal and social significance.

9

Part of this study was done under a grant from the Joint Awards Council of the State University of New York Research Foundation. I wish to express gratitude to Lawrence Pollinger, Ltd., D. H. Lawrence's literary executors, to the Humanities Research Center of the University of Texas, and to the Bancroft Library of the University of California at Berkeley for the opportunity to examine Lawrence's manuscripts, and to the estate of the Late Mrs. Frieda Lawrence, Cambridge University Press, and Lawrence Pollinger, Ltd. for permission to excerpt passages from the manuscript of the unpublished seventh chapter of *Etruscan Places*. An early version of the chapter on *Twilight in Italy* appeared in *The D. H. Lawrence Review*, Summer 1974, and an early version of the final chapter appeared in *Essays in Literature*, Fall 1976; I am grateful for the editors' permission to publish revised versions here. James C. Cowan, W. J. Keith, and Keith Sagar provided help at crucial stages of my project. I particularly thank Samuel Hynes and Van Akin Burd for their aid and advice, and Raymond G. Malbone for his very helpful reading of the manuscript. Finally, I wish to express gratitude to my wife Carol for her encouragement and especially for her comradeship in our pursuit of Lawrence's Etruscans.

Cortland, New York, 1980

CHAPTER I

Mind and World

D. H. Lawrence's travel books *Twilight in Italy, Sea and Sardinia, Mornings in Mexico* and *Etruscan Places* reward close study not merely because they were written by one of the most important figures in modern literature, but because they are the consciously structured, fully articulated works of the imagination that come closest to expressing Lawrence himself: the complex human being known to his friends and acquaintances and revealed in his letters. Paul Morel, Rupert Birkin, Richard Lovat Somers, and other protagonists of the novels and stories, while they are to one extent or another projections of Lawrence, are still characters in carefully constructed fictions. The writer of the essays is Lawrence in the role of analyst and teacher. In spite of Lawrence's insistence on the autobiographical nature of his poetry,[1] the writing of poems even so personal as "Piano," "Song of a Man Who Has Come Through," and "The Ship of Death" involved the process of distancing that criticism has labelled with the term "persona." Lawrence as he is reflected in his four travel books is the closest literary approximation we have to the man himself in his personal complexity and in his changing responses to the physical and imaginative worlds in which he lived. David Cavitch has observed that Lawrence "believed that traveling aided his discovery and fulfillment." Cavitch quotes Rawdon Lilly of the novel *Aaron's Rod*: "A new place brings out a new thing in a man."[2] He neglects, however, to quote Aaron Sisson's response: "The man in the middle of you doesn't change."[3]

The travel books reflect the effects that Lawrence's journeys seem to have had on his intellectual and emotional makeup, but they also help us to recognize the "man in the middle" of him and the consistency that underlies the apparent contradictions implicit in the other works of various phases of his career. They give evidence of his recognition of the central tension in himself—and in modern Western man—between the attractions of the mind and those of the senses, anticipation of the future and nostalgia for the past, the experience of the community and that of the individual. They illuminate two conflicts that are fundamental to all of Lawrence's writing. The first is that between his prophet-like impulse to impose an ideal order on the perception of experience and on human behaviour, and the sensitivity to the realities of life that led him to resist such an imposition of order and celebrate its opposite. Baruch Hochman has observed that Lawrence "oscillates between an atomistic sense of the radical claims of the pre-conscious, pre-social self in its isolation, and a totalitarian sense of the validity of civilization."[4] The word "oscillates" suggests a capricious shifting between conflicting sets of beliefs, but Lawrence's thought was characterized, rather, by a continuous attempt, at times conscious and at times apparently not, to find a reconciliation for seemingly contradictory impulses. Lawrence was aware that he sometimes overstated his case, usually in favour of the "pre-conscious, pre-social self." In a 1928 letter to Earl Brewster, Lawrence wrote of *Lady Chatterley's Lover*, "it's a novel of the phallic Consciousness: or the phallic Consciousness *versus* the mental-spiritual Consciousness: and of course you know which side I take. The *versus* is not my fault: there should be no *versus*. The two things must be reconciled in us. But now they're daggers drawn."[5] The second conflict in Lawrence's writing is an expression of the first: it is a conflict between the vision of creative community fostered by the prophetic mind and the emphasis on individual experience and individualism that resulted from his sense of the world's spontaneity and complexity. These opposing forces were not always equally matched in their struggle for dominance over Lawrence's imagination, and the travel books illustrate, perhaps more clearly than any of Lawrence's other writings, their relative strength in different periods of his career and the changes of mind and feeling that he underwent in relation to them. The travel books often anticipate and always clarify the expressions of these changes in Lawrence's novels, stories, and poems.

I have been referring to Lawrence's collections of essays on Italy and Mexico as travel books, but they are not travel books in the usual sense. There is, of course, a large body of English travel literature preceding Lawrence, from the Renaissance accounts of voyages of discovery to the eighteenth and nineteenth century diaries and commentaries of professional travelers, colonizers, and adventurers, and literary men like Smollet, Trollope, Butler, and Kipling. But the aim of these predecessors seems primarily to have been to provide their readers with vicarious experience of unfamiliar places and cultures or to help them prepare for similar physical journeys. Lawrence's aims, by contrast, were deeper, more personal, and more ambitious. The first was to capture on paper something of the elusive quality he called "the spirit of place."

> Every continent has its own great spirit of place. Every people is polarized in some particular locality, which is home, the homeland. Different places on the face of the earth have different vital effluence, different

12

chemical exhalation, different polarity with different stars: call it what you like. But the spirit of the place is a great reality.[6]

In a discussion of the place of Lawrence's travel books in the history of the genre, Billy T. Tracy points out that in his acute sense of place Lawrence was, like John Millington Synge and W. H. Hudson, "alert ... to those moments when landscape transformed the consciousness of the observer." Tracy continues, "Certain landscapes enabled the Irish playwright and the La Platan naturalist to shed their modern outlooks and enter a more primitive world."[7] John Alcorn, writing of the concept of spirit of place, links Lawrence with contemporaries of his such as Hudson and H. M. Tomlinson, calling them "naturists." The naturist "sees man as part of an animal continuum; he reasserts the importance of instinct as a key to human happiness; he tends to be suspicious of the life of the mind; he is wary of abstractions."[8] Alcorn sees the emphasis in naturist travel writing on primitive or relatively unsophisticated societies' interactions with their natural surroundings and the relative indifference in such writing to the cathedrals, museums, and historical sites that dominate conventional travel literature as being "essentially a literary means of probing into non-conceptual and instinctive areas of human experience."[9] Lawrence's second aim in his travel books was closely related to his exploration of the spirit of place: through discovering his reactions to unfamiliar places to discover himself "a new man," and so to articulate his sense of the nature of the individual's place—and potential—in the modern world.

Lawrence's travel books are essays in the root sense of the word: *attempts.* Each takes its form from the life-experience it describes. *Sea and Sardinia* and *Etruscan Places* are closer, in their geographical-chronological principles of organization, to conventional travel literature than are *Twilight in Italy* and *Mornings in Mexico*, but all four take their inner forms not from the journeys themselves but from the interaction of Lawrence's sensibility with the places and modes of life he encountered. Although the tension between future and past, mind and senses, and community and individualism is central to all four, each book is a fresh response to experience, a new attempt to balance Lawrence's antithetical turn of mind against the realities that confronted him in Italy, Sardinia, Mexico, and New Mexico. *Twilight in Italy* and *Mornings in Mexico* are structured thematically, while their surface textures are anecdotal. In these two books Lawrence selected among the sights, events, and encounters of several months and reorganized them to bring out the essential qualities of the Italian, Mexican, and New Mexican Indian cultures and of his own responses to them. *Sea and Sardinia* recounts

13

a week's travels almost in the manner of a diary, but the book's casual tone is deceptive: Lawrence's comments and reflections turn it into an account of an unsuccessful spiritual pilgrimage. While *Etruscan Places* also follows the outlines of an actual excursion, it is above all an evocation of dormant qualities of consciousness which Lawrence sought to reawaken in his readers.

Lawrence's four travel books are much more than introductions to places: they are statements, often seminal statements, of the directions taken by Lawrence's imagination. *Twilight in Italy* points the way toward the analysis of modern European civilization to which Lawrence gave fictional expression in *The Rainbow* and *Women in Love*. *Sea and Sardinia* reveals the longings and foretells the frustrations that were later embodied in the "leadership" novels of *Aaron's Rod*, *Kangaroo*, and *The Plumed Serpent*. *Mornings in Mexico* and *Etruscan Places* indicate the new direction that Lawrence was to take in the works of his final years, particularly *Lady Chatterley's Lover*, *The Escaped Cock*, and *Last Poems*. But more importantly the travel books are expressions, at first tentative and ambiguous but increasingly vigorous and definitive, of the patterns that Lawrence saw underlying human experience.

Several critics have put forward the idea that Lawrence's travel books represent stages in a "spiritual quest." John Alcorn observes that the story of the typical "naturist travel book is, in fact, the story of a search for Eden."[10] Ronald Weiner calls Lawrence's travel books "rhetorically molded fables of the modern sensibility in search of unspoiled being."[11] Edward Nehls identifies in them a search for a society "in which blood and intellect were in balance," a location for Rananim, the community Lawrence sometimes dreamed of founding.[12] The name for the colony, which Lawrence at various times hoped to establish somewhere in England, in Florida, in the Pacific, in South America, and in New Mexico, was derived from the Hebrew of Psalm 33, "Rejoice, O ye righteous in the Lord," which his friend S. S. Koteliansky was fond of chanting. Lawrence's conception of Rananim varied, often in response to his friends' and acquaintances' reactions to his plans, but his most detailed discussion of it is contained in a letter written in 1915 to Lady Ottoline Morrell, who he hoped at that time might co-operate in its realization.

> I want you to form the nucleus of a new community which shall start a new life amongst us—a life in which the only riches is integrity of character. So that each one may fulfill his own nature and deep desires to the utmost, but wherein tho', the ultimate satisfaction and joy is in the completeness of us all as one. . . . I hold this the most sacred duty—the gathering together of a number of people who shall so agree to live by the *best*

14

they know, that they shall be *free* to live by the best they know. The ideal, the religion, must now be *lived, practised*. We will have no more *churches*. We will bring church and house and shop together. I do believe that there are enough decent people to make a start with. Let us get the people.[13]

The frequency and extremity of Lawrence's vacillations concerning the viability of Rananim can be seen by comparing two letters to Koteliansky written early in 1916. The first is dated January 6.

Well, I am willing to believe that there isn't any Florida ... There is my ultimate art, and my thoughts, as you say. Very good, so be it. It is enough, more than enough, if they will only leave me alone. ... As for their world, it is like artificial lights that are blown out—one can only remember it. I can't see it or hear it or feel it any more—it must be all blown out to extinction. There is another world, a sort of rarer reality: a world with thin, clear air and untouched skies, that have not been looked at nor covered with smoke. There is another world, which I prefer. And I don't care about any people, none, so long as they won't try to claim attention from me.[14]

Less than two months later, on February 25, Lawrence wrote, "We must add all our strength together, all of us, to win a new world, a new being all together; it is not enough to have being individually, we must have a true being in common."[15] The Rananim idea came to the surface again several times when Lawrence thought he had found congenial companions, as in 1923 when Lawrence was living near Taos, New Mexico.[16] But Knud Merrild, who with Kai Gotzsche, a fellow Danish painter, lived near the Lawrences, remembered that Lawrence always drew back at the thought of making Rananim a reality.

Sometimes he wanted this new life movement to be a colony, but when we began to discuss it in detail, he got scared. "Too many people," he said. The colony idea was then reduced to a small group only, but when he began to mention by name some of his friends, he became highly distrustful, and the group idea was reduced to include only the Lawrences and the Danes.[17]

The connection between Lawrence's travels and his dream of Rananim is best put into perspective in his review, published in 1927, of *Gifts of Fortune*, a travel book written by Tomlinson.

We travel in order to cross seas and land on other coasts. We do not travel in order to go from one hotel to another, and see a few side-shows. We travel, perhaps, with a secret and absurd hope of setting foot on the Hesperides, of running our boat up a little creek and landing in the Garden of Eden.

This hope is always defeated. There is no Garden of Eden, and the Hesperides never were. Yet, in our very search for them, we touch the coasts of illusion, and come into contact with other worlds.[18]

It would be inaccurate to suggest that Lawrence's travel books are unrelated to his Rananim project, but to treat them as the record of a search for a congenial place in which to found a utopian community would be to oversimplify. In the "Excurse" chapter of *Women in Love*, Rupert Birkin tells Ursula Brangwen that they should "wander off" together, but that the full fruition of their love doesn't really depend upon place. "It isn't really a locality. . . . It's a perfected relation between you and me, and others—the perfect relation—so that we are free together."[19] Lawrence identified this relation, sometimes described on a personal level as a perfected internal balance, with God and godliness.

We go in search of God, following the Holy Ghost, and depending on the Holy Ghost. There is no Way. There is no Word. There is no Light. The Holy Ghost is ghostly and invisible. The Holy Ghost is nothing, if you like. Yet we hear His strange calling, the strange calling like a hound on the scent, away in the unmapped wilderness.[20]

Thus for Lawrence places were not goals but means to a goal, and his travel books do not chronicle a quixotic search for utopia. Rather, they record Lawrence's moments of contact with "other worlds." They reveal the ways in which his concept of community and its relation to felt experience evolved in the course of his career. They recount his search for a creative mode of living in the industrial age and for a way to reconcile his impulses toward public action and personal fulfillment.

The distinction made by Lawrence's biographer Emile Delavenay between Lawrence as a philosopher/prophet and as an observer of present reality is useful in understanding the apparent conflict between these impulses.

Lawrence claimed that "the essential function of art is moral"; a morality, he added, "which changes the blood, not the mind": in other words he saw in literature an instrument at the service of some ambitious but vague programme for changing mankind. While the prophet in him wanted to use his art for a purpose, the poet was content with what he called "poetry of the present." That contradiction is found in all his works, to a greater degree perhaps than with any among his contemporaries who allowed the tradition of hero-worship inherited from romanticism to shade off into artist-worship. In many of his writings Lawrence treads delicately between the two, and the Lawrence legend as it exists today is also on that borderline.[21]

16

In his "Study of Thomas Hardy" Lawrence indicated his own awareness of the duality that underlay his desire to create.

> The religious effort is to conceive, to symbolize that which the human soul, or the soul of the race, lacks, that which it is not, and which it requires, yearns for. . . .

*　*　*

> Whereas the artistic effort is the effort of utterance, the supreme effort of expressing knowledge, that which has been for once, that which was enacted.[22]

The disparity between the "religious effort" and the "artistic effort," between the character of the prophet and the character of the observer-poet, or, to put it more broadly, the confrontation between the forces of mind and world, is central to the pattern of the travel books and to an understanding of Lawrence's imagination.

By "mind" I mean the elements in Lawrence's intellectual and emotional makeup which led him to try, in various contexts, to impose a conceptual order on the external world. Having formulated his "belief in the blood, the flesh, as being wiser than the intellect,"[23] he made it—or attempted to make it—the basis of a program to be followed by his sympathetic fictional characters and sometimes to be imposed by them on the people around them and the societies in which they live. Obvious examples of such characters include Rawdon Lilly in *Aaron's Rod*, Kangaroo in *Kangaroo*, Don Ramón Carrasco in *The Plumed Serpent*, and to a lesser extent Rupert Birkin in *Women in Love*. Evelyn Scott, in her *Dial* review of *Women in Love* and *The Lost Girl* (April 1921), suggested a cultural explanation for this tendency to try to turn a metaphysical system into a social program: "If Mr. Lawrence were a Russian he would take the answer to life as his art gives it, in terms of other worldliness . . . but belonging to the English race of moralists, Mr. Lawrence persists in a search for temporal solutions."[24] Psychological explanations are also possible: it may be that Lawrence's interest in turning his ideas into social or political programs reflected his desire to free himself from female domination like that exercised by his mother and attempted (if *Sons and Lovers* can be taken as evidence) by Jessie Chambers. In the novels it is Don Ramón, who like Paul Morel is freed from a woman's stifling protectiveness by her death, who comes closest to successfully projecting a Lawrentian philosophy upon society. Harry T. Moore, in a discussion of Lawrence and homosexuality, has suggested that in his "celebrations of maleness"—particularly in *The Plumed Serpent*—Lawrence "may have been the frail boy ('mardarse') forever seeking a wish fulfillment of strength," adding that this

17

"was not compensation-by-identification—that is, Lawrence writing as from the point of view of physical gianthood, and by a process of introjection 'becoming' the admired strongman. . . . "[25] Yet it could be argued that Lawrence's impulse to create, in life (the Rananim plan) and in fiction, a system to be believed in and a program to be followed by others was a reaction against his awareness of his physical frailty. In any event, the impulse of "mind" was behind Lawrence's short-lived wartime lecture scheme, his letters to friends and acquaintances about Rananim, and the writing of his books on the unconscious and of essays like "The Crown," "The Reality of Peace," and "Education of the People." In his travel books this element is most obviously represented in the passages of analysis, interpretation, and exhortation which some early reviewers mistakenly dismissed as lamentable digressions from the travel writer's task of external description. It is particularly prominent in *Sea and Sardinia*, where social activity is most explicitly proposed as a means of winning freedom from the domination of the female.

By "world" I mean Lawrence's sensitivity to the realities of actual life, which often ignores or resists the order that mind would impose. This is what Hochman refers to as the "claims of the pre-conscious, pre-social self." It is the quality of conscious that reaches some of its finest expressions in the poems of *Bird, Beasts and Flowers* and that has been described so well by Aldous Huxley in the introduction to his edition of Lawrence's letters.

> To be with Lawrence was a kind of adventure, a voyage of discovery into newness and otherness. For, being himself of a different order, he inhabited a different universe from that of common men—a brighter and intenser world, of which, while he spoke, he would make you free. He looked at things with the eyes, so it seemed, of a man who had been at the brink of death and to whom, as he emerges from the darkness, the world reveals itself as unfathomably beautiful and mysterious. . . . He seemed to know, by personal experience, what it was like to be a tree or a daisy or a breaking wave or even the mysterious moon itself. He could get inside the skin of an animal and tell you in the most convincing detail how it felt and how, dimly, inhumanly, it thought.[26]

In Lawrence's novels this sensitivity to external reality is evidenced in his perceptive landscapes and cityscapes. It is embodied in Ursula Brangwen, who refuses to accept Birkin's idealized "star-equilibrium" and leads him to a more conventional but more human mode of relationship;[27] in Aaron Sisson, who draws back from Lilly's conscious program of leadership and submission; in Richard Lovat Somers' ultimate recognition that he cannot submerge his identity in a mass movement; and in Kate Leslie, whose final acceptance of Don Ramón and Don Cipriano rests on a personal attraction while she reserves judgment on the Quetzalcoatl religion which they seek to impose on Mexico and on her. It is this resistance to final formulation and this openness to felt experience of the world that account for the ambivalence which characterized the writer of the travel books—for Lawrence was himself a compound of Birkin and Ursula, Lilly and Sisson, Don Ramón and Kate Leslie.

The central conflict in Lawrence's travel books and, as they illuminate it, all of Lawrence's writing, is between the vision of community fostered by the prophetic mind and the insistence upon the fundamental importance of the individual that resulted from his sense of the world's everyday realities. Some of Lawrence's ambivalence about community can perhaps be traced to his early experiences. His physical frailty and his dependence on his mother are of course well known, and "Red Herring," a bit of doggerel Lawrence included in *Pansies* (1929) suggests how her influence cut him off even as a child from relaxed participation in life outside the home.

> My father was a working man
>   and a collier was he,
> at six in the morning they turned him down
>   and they turned him up for tea.
>
> My mother was a superior soul
>   a superior soul was she,
> cut out to play a superior role
>   in the god-damn bourgeoisie.
>
> We children were the in-betweens
>   little non-descripts were we,
> indoors we called each other *you,*
>   outside, it was *tha* and *thee.*
>
> But time has fled, our parents are dead
>   we've risen in the world all three;
> but still we are in-between, we tread
>   between the devil and the deep cold sea.[28]

As a schoolboy in Eastwood Lawrence suffered under the harsh discipline of the master and from the taunts of the other boys, who considered him effeminate. Later, as a commuting student at Nottingham High School, he had little opportunity to participate in its social life, and he was looked down upon because he was the son of a collier. His Director at Haywood's, the Nottingham surgical appliance factory where he worked briefly in 1901, remembered him as being "very quiet and reserved," having "very little to say in conversation, both in work time and outside."[29] The young Lawrence formed close personal friendships (most notably with Jessie Chambers, the original of Miriam in *Sons and Lovers*, her brother Alan, and George Neville, a fellow High School student from Eastwood) but was uncomfortable in large formal groups. He could respond to the pleasures of community, as he did among the "Pagans," the apprentice teachers who travelled together between Eastwood and Ilkeston from 1903 to 1905,[30] but Lawrence saw formal institutions as being arbitrary, confining, and potentially destructive of self-respect. In his study of Hardy, Lawrence analyzed the earlier novelist's works in terms of his own inner conflict.

> This is the tragedy [in Hardy], and only this: . . . first, that he is a member of the community, and must, upon his honour, in no way move to disintegrate the community, either in its moral or its practical form; second, that the convention of the community is a prison to his natural, individual desire, a desire that compels him, whether he feels justified or not, to break the bounds of the community, lands him outside the pale, there to stand alone, and say: "I was right, my desire was real and inevitable; if I was to be myself I must fulfill it, convention or no convention," or else, there to stand alone, doubting, and saying: "Was I right, was I wrong? If I was wrong, oh, let me die!"—in which case he courts death.[31]

Lawrence, either consciously or unconsciously, chose a third course of action: to acknowledge the conflict between his need for community and his need for separateness and work it out dynamically in his writing. In Lawrence's works the impulse to community is often overbalanced by its opposite.[32] Community sometimes triumphs on the conceptual level, as in *The Plumed Serpent*, but in Lawrence the life experience is finally shown to be rooted in the individual, and civilization is shown to have validity—or potential validity—only insofar as it contributes to the individual's fulfillment. At the end of *Women in Love* Birkin stubbornly insists upon his vision of something beyond the conventional marital relation, but he lives with Ursula in a union of two still-separate individuals like that celebrated in the closing poems of *Look! We Have Come Through!*. In *Kangaroo*, as I have pointed out, Somers abandons politics for the sake of the intellectual, spiritual, and personal freedom that he feels can only be maintained outside the realm of collective action. In *Lady Chatterley's Lover* Mellors articulates a plan for the regeneration of English society, but the end of the novel finds him isolated on a farm in Derbyshire, looking forward to reunion with Connie—a reunion of one man and one woman. The essay "The State of Funk," written in 1929, affirms that Lawrence's ultimate interest as a writer was in individuals rather than in actual or potential social movements.

> As a novelist, I feel it is the change inside the individual which is my real concern. The great social change interests me and troubles me, but it

is not my field. I know a change is coming—and I know we must have a more generous, more human system based on the life values and not on the money values. That I know. But what steps to take I don't know. Other men know better."[33]

Last Poems, one of the final and certainly one of the finest expressions of Lawrence's imagination, shows him turning inward to seek a reconciliation that is personal and individual even though it follows a pattern suggested by Egyptian and Etruscan religious artifacts.

The critic F. von Broembsen suggests that the great difficulty in reaching an understanding of Lawrence's thought is that in his "fictional lifeworld" Lawrence rejects the very basis of Western culture: "the individual as a soul engaged in creative evolution."[34] The examples I have cited would seem to contradict Broembsen's assertion, but in fact they do not. "Individualism" and "freedom" are not social issues for Lawrence. One does not *achieve* individuality; as a living creature he *has* it by definition. Everyone, every thing, is separate and unique. Similarly, as John Alcorn puts it, in Lawrence's view "freedom of the individual is not a gift of civilization, and exists prior to culture, not because of it."[35] Broembsen explains that Lawrence and his characters do not seek to achieve individuality in the accepted sense of the word. Rather, they pursue the fulfillment of a *role* appropriate to their radical selfhood. The societies in which they live offer Birkin, Somers, and Mellors no such roles. Broembsen cites Don Ramón as the best example of a Lawrentian character who finds—or rather fashions—an appropriate role; yet even he, because like Lawrence he straddles the modern world of the self-conscious ego and the primitive world of unconscious being, is ambivalent about his inevitable fate, as the incarnation of Quetzalcoatl, of scapegoat.[36] The conflict in Ramón is an expression of the conflict in Lawrence between the assertion of individuality *in the usual sense* (which is, paradoxically, an aspect of the impulse I have called "mind") and the development of true individuality, selfhood within the community (an aspect of "world"). This conflict finds some measure of resolution in Lawrence's later works, particularly *Etruscan Places*, where he envisions a type of community, very different from our modern democracies and dictatorships, in which the individual could take part without sacrificing his selfhood. The special significance of Lawrence's travel books is that they chart the course —generally in advance of his fiction and poetry—of his changing responses to, and his approach toward a reconciliation of, the demands of mind and world.

Lawrence's circumnavigation of the globe is not fully reflected in the subjects of his travel books; for his experiences in England, Germany, Ceylon, and Australia one must look to his novels, stories, plays, poems, letters, and other non-fiction writings. But psychologically and philosophically the four books describe a circle or, as Lawrence called it in *Mornings in Mexico* and in his first essay on Herman Melville in *Studies in Classic American Literature*, a swerve or curve of return toward primitive modes of perception but ultimately onward into the future. Lawrence discusses Melville's fascination, recorded in *Omoo*, with the life of the South Sea Islanders and his ultimate revulsion against it.

> And your own soul will tell you that however false and foul our own forms and systems are now, still, through the many centuries since Egypt, we have been living and struggling forwards along some road that is no road, yet it is a great life-development. We have struggled on, and on we must still go. We may have to smash things. Then let us smash. And our road may have to take a great swerve, that seems a retrogression.
>
> But we can't go back. Whatever else the South Sea Islander is, he is centuries and centuries behind us in the life-struggle, the consciousness struggle, the struggle of the soul into fullness. . . .
>
> *   *   *
>
> We can't go back. We can't go back to the savages: not a stride. We can be in sympathy with them. We can take a great curve in their direction, onwards. But we cannot turn the current of our life backwards, back towards their soft warm twilight and uncreate mud. Not for a moment.[37]

Lawrence felt the need for such a curve of return very directly and imperatively in the course of his trip to Sardinia. He reflects in *Sea and Sardinia* on how travel in Italy "is like a most fascinating act of self-discovery—back, back down the old ways of time." But Sardinia makes him realize that life is "not only a process of rediscovering backwards."

> It is that, also: and it is that intensely. Italy has given me back I know not what of myself, but a very, very great deal. She has found for me so much that was lost: like a restored Osiris. But this morning in the omnibus I realise that, apart from the great discovery backwards, which one *must* make before one can be whole at all, there is a move forwards. There are unknown, unworked lands where the salt has not lost its savour. But one must have perfected oneself in the great past first. (*SS*, 216, 123, 122-23)

The curve of return toward the primitive past would make possible the revitalization of the radical, unconscious self, able now to withstand and perhaps refashion the "fallen" mechanistic world of the present.

Lawrence's path in the travel books runs from his concern, in *Twilight in Italy*, with defining the nature and potential of man in the modern world, through his search for a collective expression of his religious impulses—involving the exploration of the possibility of participation in primitive modes of life—to a recognition that an actual reversion to such modes is impossible and a realization that the individual as he exists in the present, curving back toward the past to gain a humanizing balance but inevitably moving onward into an indefinite future, must be the foundation for any new relation of men to each other and of mankind to the universe. The first three books are essentially diagnostic. *Twilight in Italy* (1916) describes Lawrence's reaction to the confrontation in rural Italy between the modern world of reason and instrumentality and the ancient world of spontaneous being, and reflects in its manner and content the tension in Lawrence himself between modern "northern" intellect and primitive "southern" sensuality. *Sea and Sardinia* (1921) presents Lawrence's self-conscious, contradictory, and unsuccessful attempt to embrace the European past as a substantive basis for contemporary action. *Mornings in Mexico* (1927), in contrast to *The Plumed Serpent*, the other major work based on Lawrence's experience of America, expresses his recognition of the radical incompatibility of modern linear, rational consciousness and the primitive cyclical, sensual consciousness. *Etruscan Places* (1932) is not a diagnosis but a tentative prescription. It is an imaginative projection of Lawrence's view of the roles of communal and personal experience upon a mysterious dead civilation. It explores the possibility—Lawrence would say the necessity—of resolving the quest for meaning first on a personal level, by putting aside modern mindfulness in order to recapture the spontaneous sense of wonder known to the American Indians and the ancient Etruscans.

Taken together, Lawrence's travel books describe the apparent contradictions and reveal the underlying consistency of his world-view. Lawrence's career as a writer was an attempt to balance and integrate the demands of mind and world: the impulse to reveal, like a prophet, the transcendent meaning of life, and the impulse to record, as an artist, the imminent meanings of the things around him. The travel books give us an intimate picture of Lawrence's journey from a recognition of the conflict between mental consciousness and sensual awareness to a sense of the possibility of resolving that conflict by following the curve of return.

CHAPTER II

The Two Infinites

The essays in *Twilight in Italy* were conceived and first written during one
of the most crucial and most productive periods in Lawrence's life: the
months he spent at Gargnano in Northern Italy in late 1912 and early 1913
after leaving England with Frieda Weekley.[1] It was in these months that
Lawrence completed the final draft of *Sons and Lovers*, wrote most of the
poems of *Look! We Have Come Through!*, and began *The Sisters*, the novel
that was to become *The Rainbow* and *Women in Love*; it was in these
months that Lawrence established the conceptual basis of the works of his
maturity. *Twilight in Italy* gives exposition and embodiment to the conflict
that underlies almost all of Lawrence's subsequent writings.

The source of this conflict or polarity, according to Lawrence, is in the
existence of two "infinites," which can be represented as "the Father and
Son, the Dark and the Light, the Senses and and the Mind, the Soul and
the Spirit, the self and the not-self, the Eagle and the Dove, the Tiger and
the Lamb." Lawrence insists that these opposing absolute principles are
equal and universal. Both infinites are potential in all human beings, and
the goal of the individual should be to bring both to realization.

> The consumation of man is twofold, in the Self and in Selflessness. By
> great retrogression back to the source of darkness in me, the Self, deep in
> the senses, I arrive at the Original, Creative Infinite. By projection forth
> from myself, I arrive at the Ultimate Infinite, Oneness in the Spirit. They
> are two Infinites, twofold approach to God. And man must know both.
>
> (*TI*, 81; 46; 58)

It is not surprising that Lawrence should have found a dualistic view of
reality congenial: it is a mode of thinking that is at least as old as Western
civilization, and one that was common to much of what he read as a young
man. Lawrence had begun to read William Blake as early as 1905,[2] and the
dualism outlined in the passage above bears a resemblance to that reflected
in Blake's *Marriage of Heaven and Hell*. By 1908 Lawrence had at least
some familiarity of the writings of Hegel, Schopenhauer, and Nietzsche, all
of whom may have influenced his dialectical approach.[3] Furthermore, the
very landscape in which Lawrence grew up could be perceived as being po-
larized between the natural (which he identified with the Self) and the

mechanical (in Lawrence's terms a manifestation of the Spirit). In 1926 he wrote of the view from the house on Walker Street in Eastwood where he had lived from 1891 to 1902, "I know that view better than any in the world."[4] In the foreground were the rather sordid miners' dwellings of The Breach; beyond them Brinsley, Moorgreen, and High Park collieries and the railroad tracks that connected them to the main line; and in the distance, beautiful rolling farmland and some remnants of Sherwood Forest. "So that the life was a curious cross between industrialism and the old agricultural England of Shakespeare and Milton and Fielding and George Eliot."[5]

What is striking is the extent to which a dualism of self and spirit underlay almost everything Lawrence wrote in his maturity. Perhaps it is too simplistic to attribute the obsessiveness of this dualism to Lawrence's feelings about his parents, but all accounts of Arthur and Lydia Lawrence suggest that they virtually embodied the opposing principles that became fundamental to their son's sense of the world. Lawrence's mother was as reserved, intellectual, future-oriented, and spiritual as his father was direct, spontaneous, present-oriented, and physical. *Sons and Lovers* attests to Lawrence's early sympathy with his mother's values, but as he gained the perspective of time Lawrence was more and more able to acknowledge the worth of his father's mode of life, especially the "dark intimacy" of the mines and the "instinct of beauty" of the miners.[6] Even in *Sons and Lovers* Walter Morel emerges as a more positive figure than Lawrence could have intended during the novel's writing. In that novel, and in Arthur and Lydia Lawrence's life, the representatives of body and spirit were in constant, apparently irreconcilable conflict, just as in Lawrence's theory the principles of Self and Spirit are in eternal tension. Lawrence's belief in these two infinites and his sense of the need for the realization of both may stem, in part, from a desire to come to an understanding of the human conflict that cast a shadow over his childhood and youth. With ample precedent in literature and philosophy, he projected that conflict upon his view of the world at large.

In *Twilight in Italy* the polarity of the two infinites is expressed in three significant ways: in the pairings of South and North, past and future, and body and spirit. But the book reveals another duality: Lawrence's alternation between spontaneity and intellection in his writing—an expression of the competing impulses of world and mind. Emile Delavenay, agreeing with earlier critics, has noted this dichotomy with disapproval: "often obscure ideas intrude into descriptions of Italian scenes which had [by the writing of the book's final version] become a distant and inaccessible mirage."[7] However, the apparent discontinuity in content and expression and the resulting tension in the texture of the work are in fact essential to the form and mean-

25

ing of *Twilight in Italy*. The interplay of descriptive and expository passages makes the book a whole that encompasses the two infinites.

There are two versions of *Twilight in Italy*. During and shortly after Lawrence's stay at Gargnano on the Lago di Garda, he published "Christs in the Tirol" in the *Saturday Westminster Gazette* (22 March 1913) and "Italian Studies: By the Lago di Garda" in the *English Review* (September 1913); these were revised in 1915 to become the four opening chapters of *Twilight in Italy*. As Delavenay has observed, the 1913 articles are particularly notable for their immediacy of descriptive style.[8] They exemplify the esthetic principles that Lawrence outlined in his 1918 essay "Poetry of the Present."

> Life, the ever-present, knows no finality, no finished crystalization. The perfect rose is only a running flame, emerging and flowing off, and never in any sense at rest, static, finished. Herein lies its transcendent loveliness. The whole tide of all life and all time suddenly heaves, and appears before us as an apparition, a revelation. We look at the very white quick of nascent creation. . . .
> This is the unrestful, ungraspful poetry of the sheer present, poetry whose very permanency lies in its wind-like transit.[9]

These pieces, like all of Lawrence's travel writings, convey a sense of the immediate encounter between the writer and the world with which he comes into contact: the heavily sensual crucifixes of the Tyrol, the beautiful Italian sunsets, the comic behaviour of an Italian *padrone* struggling with an American doorspring, the English traveller's surprise at a performance of *Hamlet* by Italian peasant actors. These descriptions of sights and events exemplify the aspect of Lawrence's writing which I have identified with the term "world": spontaneous response to immediate experience.

For the book's final version, these first four essays had been revised and interlaced with passages of philosophical and political theory. In other words, "mind" began to intrude. Still, it would be misleading to think of the theoretical passages as irrelevant excrescences; they seem rather to be later extrapolations of ideas that had occurred to Lawrence at the times of the incidents recounted in the essays. For example, Lawrence's long discussion in *Twilight in Italy* of Hamlet's "To be or not to be" soliloquy (*TI*, 127-33; 70-73; 91-95) did not appear in the 1913 "Italian Studies," but in a letter to Ernest Collings written the day after the performance he described there Lawrence wrote in words that prefigure those of the book, "We are Hamlet without the Prince of Denmark. We cannot *be*. 'To be or not to be'—it is the question with us now, by Jove. And nearly every Englishman says 'Not to be.' So he goes in for Humanitarianism and suchlike forms of not-being."[10] Thus the theoretical passages that were added after the "Italian Studies" version was published probably do fairly closely reflect the nature of Lawrence's thinking at the time of his stay in Gargnano. It may be that with the coming of the First World War and in the face of what Lawrence saw at that time as the imminent collapse of the contemporary social structure he felt the need to express his conception of the ailments of Western civilization more explicitly than he had in the original version.

Criticism of *Twilight in Italy* has insisted on the discontinuity between the descriptive and theoretical passages. Like Delavenay, John Middleton Murry, Richard Aldington, and the contemporary *Times Literary Supplement* reviewer have seen *Twilight in Italy* as a potentially fine travel book which has been spoiled by philosophizing; Aldington goes so far as to suggest that some readers should probably skip over the more theoretical passages.[11] Mark Schorer, on the other hand, sees the intellectual dimension as the essential unifying factor in Lawrence's travel books.[12] Both points of view are only partially correct. The interest and significance of *Twilight in Italy* lie in the very juxtaposition of the two styles, reflecting as it does the tension between the two "infinites" of body and spirit. In *Twilight in Italy* spontaneous, often lyrical responses to perceived experience are balanced against analyses of and generalizations from that experience. As I have indicated, these analyses deal with three interrelated polarities: racial (the contrast between South and North), societal (past and future), and religious or metaphysical (body and spirit). Each of these polarities is established at the narrative-descriptive as well as the expository level of the book, so that each contributes to Lawrence's fundamental theme of tension between the two infinites.

The racial polarity is the most striking, and has been somewhat controversial. Delavenay has asserted that the final version of *Twilight in Italy* constituted a platform for "a corporatist, authoritarian and mystic State, not exempt from philo-Teutonic racialism."[13] This is an exaggeration. It is true that the concept of "racial" or "national" characteristics is implicit in the book, but Lawrence never translated this concept into a coherent political philosophy. He was, however, conscious of the book's identification of nations and peoples with certain predelictions or tendencies. In a letter to Lady Cynthia Asquith written in 1915, he described *Twilight in Italy* as "a book of sketches, about the nations, Italian and German, and English, full of philosophizing and struggling to show things real."[14] In the opening chapter, "The Crucifix Across the Mountains," Lawrence describes his journey along the "imperial road" across the Alps and reflects on the Holy Roman Empire:

Maybe a certain Grossenwahn is inherent in the German nature. If only nations would realize that they have certain natural characteristics, if only

27

they could understand and agree to each other's particular nature, how much simpler it would all be. (*TI*, 3; 3; 3)

Lawrence's basic distinction in this regard is between the southern and northern nations, and particularly between Italian sensuality and English intellectuality. In "The Lemon Gardens," the second chapter of the "Lago di Garda" section, Lawrence focuses on the darkness of Italian interiors, seeing them as symbolic of the "senses made absolute." Lawrence traces the contrast in national character to the Renaissance, when Italy, as represented by Michaelangelo (*TI*, 59; 34; 42-43), turned back to the Hebrew and Greek emphasis on the body, while Northern Europe continued the Medieval movement toward the spirit.

> What is that which parted ways with the terrific eagle-like angel of the senses at the Renaissance? The Italians said, "We are one in the Father: we will go back." The Northern races said, "We are one in Christ: we will go on." (*TI*, 64; 37; 46)

The northern movement, according to Lawrence, was away from the direct, sensual affirmation of the self and toward the intellectual affirmation of the not-self: man in the abstract, man seen empirically.

> It was this religious belief [in the transcendence of personal limitation] which expressed itself in science. Science was the analysis of the outer self, the outer world. And the machine is the great reconstructed selfless power. Hence the active worship to which we were given at the end of the last century, the worship of mechanized force. (*TI*, 70-71; 40; 50)

Illustrations of this contrast between the Italian and northern, particularly English, national characters appear throughout both the original and final versions of Lawrence's Italian essays. In the final section of the 1913 "Italian Studies," Lawrence compares the behavior of the Gargnano audience during and after a performance of "Amleto" with that of a typical English audience.

> The people of the audience are a joy for ever. It is free and united as a tea-party downstairs. In English theatres every man seems to have an abnormal sensitiveness in his knees and his elbows, and he keeps himself contracted as tight as he can, so as not to touch his neighbor. Here the men lounge and lean on one another, talk and laugh and stroll, or stare in utter childish absorption, so that the place seems full of pleasure for everybody, and everybody shares with everybody else. It gives a warm feeling of life.[15]

The Italians are warm, easygoing, and sensual, while the northern races are cold and restrained. In the corresponding section of *Twilight in Italy* Law-

28

rence describes an Italian performance of Ibsen's *Ghosts*, but his comparison of the text of Ibsen's play with the Italian interpretation shows that he feels that both approaches are incomplete and inadequate. For Lawrence the northern attitude toward sexuality is overly intellectual, but the southern attitude is overbalanced in the opposite direction.

> Ibsen is exciting, nervously sensational. But this was really moving, a real crying in the night. One loved the Italian nation, and wanted to help it with all one's soul. But when one sees the perfect Ibsen, how he hates the Norwegian and Swedish nations! They are detestable.
>
> They seem to be fingering with the mind the secret places and sources of the blood, impertinent, irreverent, nasty. . . . It is with them a sort of phallic worship also, but now the worship is mental and perverted: the phallus is the real fetish, but it is the source of uncleanliness and corruption and death, it is the Moloch, worshipped in obscenity.
>
> Which is unbearable. The phallus is a symbol of creative divinity. But it represents only part of creative divinity. The Italian has made it represent the whole. Which is now his misery, for he has to destroy his symbol in himself. (*TI*, 108-09; 61; 78)

In "The Dance" at San Gandenzio, Lawrence depicts an encounter between an Italian woodcutter and an English gentlewoman that anticipates the confrontation between English restraint and southern sensuality in *The Lost Girl*.

> He is like a god, a strange natural phenomenon, most ultimate and compelling, wonderful.
>
> But he is not a human being. The woman, somewhere shocked in her independent soul, begins to fall away from him. She has another being, which he has not touched, and which she will fall back upon.
>
> (*TI*, 182; 99-100; 129)

This polarity extends even to the landscape; perhaps it is partly a function of landscape, a result of the influence of the "spirit of place." In the final chapter of *Twilight in Italy* Lawrence describes his descent from the Gotthard pass on the way back from a walking tour in Switzerland.

> It is strange how different the sun-dried, ancient southern slopes of the world are, from the northern slopes. It is as if the god Pan really had his home among these sun-bleached stones and tough, sun-dark trees.
>
> (*TI*, 299-300; 163; 207)

But Lawrence's attitude toward the components of this North-South polarity remains ambivalent. I have noted his appreciation of the insouciance of the Italian audience, an expression of the unself-conscious sensuality he characterizes as "phallic." In "The Lemon Gardens" he admits his attraction

29

to the Italian way of life: "This, then, is the secret of Italy's attraction for us, this phallic worship. To the Italian the phallus is the symbol of individual creative immortality, to each man his own Godhead" (*TI*, 78; 44; 56). By "individual," of course, Lawrence means here the individual in his primal, unself-conscious state, not the modern individual who seeks constantly to find objective self-definition and self-justification. In the famous letter to Ernest Collings in which Lawrence affirms his belief in "the blood, the flesh, as being wiser than the intellect," he explains, "That is why I like to live in Italy. The people are so unconscious. They only feel and want: they don't know. We know too much."[16] Still, Lawrence almost automatically acknowledges the "superiority" of the northern position.

> Wherein are we superior? Only because we went beyond the phallus in search of the Godhead, the creative origin. And we found the physical forces and the secrets of science. (*TI*, 78; 44-45; 56)

Knowing Lawrence's antipathy to modern science we can see that this, too, is a qualified acceptance. Lawrence sees Italian phallicism and northern rationalism as manifestations of the two infinites, neither of which should be asserted as being superior to the other: but it is necessary to recognize the difference between them. The great mistake of the northern nations is in attempting to combine them by bending the forces of the body to the will of the intellect or, conversely, by using the creations of the intellect in the service of irrational impulses which we disguise as selflessness—a behavior which, Lawrence implies, is responsible for the horrors of modern war.

> We continue to give service to Selfless God, we worship the great selfless oneness in the spirit, oneness in service of the great humanity, that which is Not-Me. This selfless God is He Who works for all alike, without consideration. And His image is the machine which dominates and cows us, we cower before it, we run to serve it. For it works for all humanity alike.
>
> At the same time, we want to be warlike tigers. That is the horror: the confusing of the two ends. We warlike tigers fit ourselves out with machinery, and our blazing tiger wrath is emitted through a machine. It is a horrible thing to see machines hauled about by tigers, at the mercy of tigers, forced to express the tiger. It is a still more horrible thing to see tigers caught up and entangled and torn in machinery. It is horrible, a chaos beyond chaos, an unthinkable hell. (*TI*, 71-72; 41; 51)

These are hardly the words of a proto-fascist, philo-Teutonic or otherwise. Indeed, it would be almost impossible to turn these observations into any kind of coherent political program, as we conceive of politics in the modern world. That this is true is further evidenced by Lawrence's confusion and vacillation in the face of specifically political manifestations. He is almost inarticulate in his attempts to discuss the Italian anarchists he meets in a Swiss factory town: "I ran down the hill in the thick Swiss darkness to the little bridge, and along the uneven cobbled street. I did not want to think, I did not want to know" (*TI*, 256; 139; 178). He cannot think about them and their future, and he cannot explain why. Lawrence seems equally ambivalent in his attitude toward Swiss democracy. The Swiss soldiers attract him:

> This little squad of Cavalry seemed more like a party of common men riding out on their own than like an army. They were very republican and very free. The officer who commanded them was one of themselves, his authority was by consent.
> It was all very pleasant and genuine; there was a sense of ease and peacefulness, quite different from the mechanical, slightly sullen maneuvering of the Germans. (*TI*, 234; 127; 163)

Yet only paragraphs later Lawrence voices his revulsion at the effects of the Swiss political system. "There is something very dead about this country. . . . One gets this feeling always in Switzerland, except high up: this feeling of average, of utter soulless ordinariness" (*TI*, 235; 128; 164).

Aldous Huxley has observed that "those who take a bird's-eye view of the world often see clearly and comprehensively, but they tend to ignore all tiresome details, all difficulties of social life, and ignoring, to judge too sweepingly and to condemn too lightly. . . . From deserts to New Mexico, from rustic Tuscany or Sicily, from the Australian bush, Lawrence observed and judged and advised the distant world of men. The judgments, as might be expected, were often sweeping and violent; the advice, though admirable as far as it went, inadequate."[17] Lawrence did take such a distant view, and practical politics were among the "tiresome details" with which he was unable to deal satisfactorily. Here is Lawrence in the book's final chapter, at an inn on the Gotthard Pass:

> I was free, in this heavy, ice-cold air, this upper world, alone. London, far away below, beyond, England, Germany, France—they were all so unreal in the night. It was a sort of grief that this continent all beneath was so unreal, false, non-existent in its activity. . . . The kingdoms of the world had no significance; what could one do but wander about?
> (*TI*, 288-89; 157; 199)

Lawrence's view in this passage is apolitical; it is the view of the artist, the immediate observer. Despite Lawrence's description of the book in his letter to Lady Cynthia Asquith, the role of "nation" or of "race" in *Twilight in Italy* is not central. It provides a conceptual framework for his reflections on

31

the opposing developmental directions of the societies he discusses and the more fundamental *human* polarity he describes in the book and in works such as the "Study of Thomas Hardy" and "The Crown."

The racial polarity, a polarity of place, is paralleled in *Twilight in Italy* by a societal polarity, which is essentially a polarity of time in which the sensual, natural past is set against a mentalized, mechanical future. As Edward Nehls has observed, "*Twilight in Italy* is made up of the two polarities of the innocent, natural world, the cycles of which are interrupted and its moral precepts ignored by man alone, and of a human world dying of a sickness for which there seems to be no ready remedy."[18] Italian society, tied to the past, is an extension of the natural component, while the society of Northern Europe represents the mechanistic future which threatens the southern Eden. But the polarity of past and future is also expressed through individuals: the old woman and the monks of Gargnano, Lawrence's landlord Pietro di Paoli, the Fiori family and the other inhabitants of San Gaudenzio, and the Italian anarchists Lawrence meets in Switzerland. Although I shall demonstrate later that this is only partly true, Lawrence seems to see the old woman, the wool-spinner of the Gargnano section, as a representative of the past. (Nehls calls her a "living anachronism" from the life "desirable" but "beyond recall."[19]) She exists outside of history, in a state preceding self-awareness.

> Her world was clear and absolute, without consciousness of self. She was not aware that there was anything in the universe except *her* universe. In her universe I was a stranger, a foreign *signore*. That I had a world of my own, other than her own, was not conceived by her. (*TI*, 39; 24; 28)

The wool-spinner and the old Italian peasant culture she represents are identified with the primitive or "original" absolute of the body, unconscious of self and of the existence of others on anything but a physical level. She is, in the distinction I have established, all "world" and no "mind." In Lawrence's schema the monks, although their life is of the past, are conceptually of the mentalized future in their abstraction from the order of reality that is so natural to the wool-spinner: "Neither the blood nor the spirit spoke in them, only the law, the abstraction of the average" (*TI*, 50; 30; 36). Their past is not the wool-spinner's primitive, sensual infinite but the past of the Middle Ages, when man sought another absolute, the affirmation of the not-self. Over the centuries, according to Lawrence, the spiritual absolute has lost its religious meaning, having been transformed into the modern penchant for mechanization and political democracy. Hence the monks, probably of peasant stock like the wool-spinner, have relinquished the absolute of the body

32

and, in the course of events, have lost the absolute of the spirit. They are merely pleasant, ineffectual men who express the soulless average.

Lawrence's contrast between the society of the past and that of the future is made clearer in his account of the *padrone*, Pietro di Paoli. He is a fallen aristrocrat, a last representative of the old feudal society, with a "naive, ancient passion to be grand" (*TI*, 55; 32; 39). An afternoon spent with Signor di Paoli serves as the occasion of Lawrence's first extended exposition of the idea that the Italian affinity with darkness, the flesh, and the senses is a link to the Mediterranean past: "It is a lapse back, back to the original position, the Mosaic position of the divinity of the flesh, and the absoluteness of its laws. . . . The mind, all the time, subserves the senses" (*TI*, 60-61; 35; 43). Although the padrone thinks of it as a longing for the future, his frustrated desire for a child is an affirmation of his affinity with the past, the flesh, the self. The real future, according to Lawrence, is the mechanicality of the northern peoples.

> Whatever we [northern people] do, it is the greater will towards self-reduction and a perfect society, analysis on the one hand, and mechanical construction on the other. This will dominates us as a whole, and until the whole breaks down, the will must persist. So that now . . . we are but attributes of the great mechanical society we have created on our way to perfection. (*TI*, 80; 45; 57)

Consciously, the *padrone* desires the mechanical future. Lawrence admires his now unprofitable lemon gardens and the bright Italian sun that shines down on them, but the *padrone* points out that "'In England you have the wealth—les richesses—you have the mineral coal and the machines, vous savez. Here we have the sun—. . . .' He wanted machines, machine production, money, and human power" (*TI*, 94; 53; 67). Here again, Lawrence's reaction is ambivalent. He recognizes the pathos of the *padrone's* longing for the machine; it is the *next* generation of Italians that will follow England into the future. But at the same time Lawrence admits that however appealing it is, the past is, after all, irrevocably past.

> I sat on the roof of the lemon-house, with the lake below and the snowy mountain opposite, and looked at the ruins on the old, olive-fuming shores, at all the peace of the ancient world still covered in sunshine, and the past seemed to me so lovely that one must look towards it, backwards, only backwards, where there is peace and beauty and no more dissonance.
> I thought of England, the great mass of London, and the black, fuming, laborious Midlands and north-country. It seemed horrible. And yet it was better than the *padrone*, this old, monkey-like cunning of fatality. It is better to go forward into error than to stay fixed inextricably in the past. (*TI*, 95; 53; 67-68)

33

The idea of the futility of an attempt to recapture the primitive past, which later led Lawrence to the concept of the curve of return, is already present in an embryonic form.

William A. Fahey has characterized the "San Gaudenzio" section of *Twilight in Italy* as a series of "little living myths";[20] it is, rather, an emblematic tableau, a carefully balanced picture of an Italy caught between the past and the future. The first chapter, "San Gaudenzio," establishes the opposition in terms of the Fiori family, the proprietors of an illegal inn which serves as the social centre of the little mountain community. "The Dance" and "Il Duro" develop the sensual, past-oriented aspect of the polarity, and "John" deals with the attraction of the intellectual-mechanical pole. The Fiori family provides an example of the duality of dark and light, body and spirit. Paolo, the father, represents the old order; Maria, his wife, the call to the future. They are like the Brangwen men and women of the opening pages of *The Rainbow*.

> Maria wanted the future, the endless possibility of life on earth. She wanted her sons to be free, to achieve a new plan of living. . . .
> Paolo was entirely remote from Maria's world. He had not yet even grasped the fact of money, not thoroughly. He reckoned in land and olive trees. So he had the old fatalistic attitude to his circumstances, even to his food. (*TI*, 158-59; 87-88; 112-13)

Giovanni, the eldest son, is the male Ursula Brangwen of this Italian Cossethay, representing the collapse of the old life and the breaking away from the land.

> He would go to America, he also. Not for anything would he stay in San Gaudenzio. His dream was to be gone. . . .
> The old order, the order of Paolo and of Pietro di Paoli, the aristocratic order of the supreme God, God the Father, the Lord, was passing away from the beautiful little territory. (*TI*, 171; 94; 121)

The pattern is repeated in the succeeding chapters. "The Dance" is an evocation of the dark sensuality of the land, in the person of the woodcutter. Faustino, the man called "Il Duro," has like Paolo Fiori been to America and returned; like Paolo he is a representative of the past, belonging as Lawrence sees it "to the god Pan, to the absolute of the senses" (*TI*, 201; 109; 141). John, a young man of the village who has also been to America, is different; he intends to return, impelled into motion into the new world.

> With his candid, open, unquestioning face, he seemed like a prisoner being conveyed from one form of life to another, or like a soul in trajectory, that has not yet found a resting-place.

What were wife and child to him?—they were the last steps of the past. His father was the continent behind him; his wife and child the foreshore of the past; but his face was set outwards, away from it all—whither, neither he nor anybody knew, but he called it America.

(*TI*, 220-21; 119; 155)

The book's final chapters further chronicle this movement toward an impersonal, disembodied future. The exiled Italian anarchists are yet another example.

I could see these sons of Italy would never go back. Men like Paolo and Il Duro broke away only to return. The dominance of the old form was too strong for them. . . . But "John" and these Italians in Switzerland were a generation younger, and they would not go back, at least not to the old Italy. Suffer as they might, and they did suffer, wincing in every nerve and fibre from the cold material insentience of the northern countries and of America, still they would endure this for the sake of something else they wanted. (*TI*, 251-52; 136-37; 176)

Lawrence's "Return Journey" shows that the attraction of the mechanized future has not only seduced the young men of Italy from their homeland; it has also invaded the landscape itself.

I walked on and on, down the Ticino valley, towards Bellinzona. The valley was perhaps beautiful: I don't know. I can only remember the road. It was broad and new, and it ran very often beside the railway. It ran also by quarries and ore factories, also through villages. And the quality of its sordidness is something that does not bear thinking of, a quality that has entered Italian life now, if it was not there before. (*TI*, 302; 146; 209)

The "twilight" of *Twilight in Italy* is emblematic of the death of the old, sensual way of life. In societal terms the book depicts—and in fact ends with —an inexorable march towards the machine. Perhaps this is why Edward Nehls called it the most depressing of Lawrence's travel books.[21] But Lawrence, with his vision of the two infinites, could hardly leave it at that, and on another level he didn't.

The major effect of the theoretical passages Lawrence added in 1915 to the Gargnano chapters was to make explicit the contrasts and polarities that were present in the 1913 articles; this is especially true of the religious or metaphysical polarity of body and spirit, being and non-being. Although there is a foreshadowing in "The Crucifix Across the Mountains," in the juxtaposition of the "mystic sensual delight" of the Bavarian peasants with the "eternal, negative radiance" of their mountain environment (*TI*, 9; 6; 7), the duality is first clearly established in the contrast between the two churches of Gargnano: San Francesco, which Lawrence describes as a

"Church of the Dove," the spirit, and San Tomasso, a "Church of the Eagle," the body. This contrast was present in the 1913 "Studies," but it is much elaborated in *Twilight in Italy*.

> The Churches of the Dove are shy and hidden: they nestle among trees, and their bells sound in the mellowness of Sunday; or they are gathered into a silence of their own in the very midst of the town, so that one passes them by without observing them. . . .
> But the Churches of the Eagle stand high, with their heads to the skies, as if they challenged the world below. They are the Churches of the Spirit of David, and their bells ring passionately, imperiously, falling on the subservient world below. (*TI*, 29-30; 19; 21-22)

At the end of the first Gargnano chapter, "The Spinner and the Monks," Lawrence discusses the problem posed by the radical discontinuity in the nature of man and his aspirations that these churches symbolize:

> Where, then, is the meeting point; where in mankind is the ecstasy of light and dark together, the supreme transcendence of the afterglow, day hovering in the embrace of the coming night like two angels embracing in the heavens, like Eurydice in the arms of Orpheus, or Persephone embraced by Pluto? (*TI*, 53; 31; 37-38)

This polarity is further explored and defined in the other Gargnano chapters, in terms of the religious implications of art. The darkness of the interior of the *padrone's* house leads Lawrence to think "of the Italian soul, how it is dark, cleaving to the eternal light. It seems to have become so, at the Renaissance" (*TI*, 58; 34; 42). Lawrence sees the art of the Middle Ages as striving toward the abstract spirituality of Christ, by the elimination of the flesh. Botticelli momentarily broke the movement, achieving a balance between body and spirit, but Michaelangelo reversed the movement, turning back toward the senses. For Michaelangelo "Christ did not exist. . . . There was God the Father, the Begetter, the Author of all flesh . . ." and according to Lawrence "this has been the Italian position ever since" (*TI*, 59; 34-35; 42-43). It was during the Renaissance that the great conflict developed, for along with Michaelangelo's assertion of the self there existed a second strain, of self-dislike and reaction against the flesh, which is represented in *Hamlet*.[22]

> The question, to be or not to be, which Hamlet puts himself, does not mean, to live or not to live. It is not the simple human being who puts himself the question, it is the supreme I, King and Father. To be or not to be King, Father, in the Self supreme? And the decision is, not to be.
> (*TI*, 127; 70; 91)

The result was "our world of Europe," which "had now really turned, swung toward a new goal, a new idea, the Infinite reached through the omission of

Self" (*TI*, 131; 72; 92), rejecting the primitive awareness of the self and embracing the modern concept of the not-self. Now, having nearly reached this goal in the abstraction of the mechanical and the institution of democracy, Europeans feel drawn again, according to Lawrence, to the other, pagan infinite, and have become a race of tigers entangled in the machines of war. Lawrence finds this development wholly unsatisfactory. It is time to pose a new question.

> To be or not to be was the question for Hamlet to settle. It is no longer our question, at least not in the same sense. When it is a question of death, the fashionable young suicide declares that his self-destruction is the final proof of his own incontrovertible being. And as for not-being in our public life, we have achieved it as much as ever we want to, as much as is necessary. Whilst in private life there is a swing back to paltry selfishness as a creed. And in the war there is the position of neutralization and nothingness. It is a question of knowing how *to be*, and how *not to be*, for we must fulfill both. (*TI*, 133; 73; 95)

Lawrence's answer is that we must learn to admit and embrace both sides of the polarity, the two infinites.

> It is past time to leave off, to cease entirely from what we are doing, and from what we have been doing for hundreds of years. It is past the time to cease seeking one infinite, ignoring, striving to eliminate the other. . . .
> There are two ways, there is not only One. There are two opposite ways to consummation. But that which relates them like the base of the triangle, this is the constant, the Absolute, this makes the Ultimate Whole. And in the Holy Spirit I know the Two Ways, the Two Infinites, the Two Consummations. And knowing the Two, I admit the Whole.
> (*TI*, 80-82; 45-47; 57-59)

The importance for Lawrence of this idea of consummation is demonstrated by its reiteration and elaboration in two essays of the wartime period, the "Study of Thomas Hardy" (written in 1914) and "The Crown" (1915). In his discussion of the treatment of the self and history in the "Hardy" study, Baruch Hochman has provided an admirable summary of that work's metaphysical schema.

> The dualism of Lawrence's system is a dualism of flesh and spirit, of female and male, of mother and father, of Father and Son. [God the Father is identified with the flesh and thus with the "female" principle, God the Son with the spirit and thus with the "male" principle.] As in the systems of nature and the psyche [which Hochman discusses earlier and which correspond loosely to *Twilight in Italy*'s place and time elements], moreover, there is a third term, in which the first two terms are

37

synthesized, or reconciled. The third term is more elusive than the first two. It is, physically and cosmically, the "being" that emerges between individuals and within individuals at the moment of consummation, when vivid life comes into being by transcending the elements of self or nature. It is the "fourth dimension" of life, that is, what "men once called heaven." It is also the "absolute" which men envision as the end of their erotic consummation, and which is both their fulfilled selves and the ideal condition toward which their selves strive. In Lawrence's trinitarian scheme, it is the "Holy Ghost."[23]

The similarities to the schema of *Twilight in Italy* should be obvious. In "The Crown," Lawrence symbolizes the polarity in terms of the creatures of the royal coat of arms. The lion, the King of Beasts, and the unicorn, the Beast of Purity, stand on opposite sides of the shield, contesting for the crown and not realizing that the crown is not the goal of the fight but its keystone.[24] In the "Hardy" study the ultimate goal is the reconciliation of opposites. Eugene Goodheart is correct, however, in observing that this is not true of all of Lawrence's speculative writing. Lawrence's wish in the "Study of Thomas Hardy" for "a fusion or a reconciliation . . . ignores his own insistence on other occasions that the two modes of being are radically and fiercely irreconcilable."[25] In "The Crown," as in *Twilight in Italy*, there is no reconciliation or synthesis but rather an affirmation of the interplay of opposites—like that between the lion and the unicorn. The consummation, "this lively body of foam, this iris between the two floods, this music between the cymbals, this supreme reason between conflicting desires, this holy spirit between the two Infinites," is only possible when both forces are present and active.

> The crown is upon the perfect balance of the fight, it is not the fruit of either victory. The crown is not the prize of either combatant. It is the *raison d'etre* of both. It is absolute within the fight. . . . it is the fight of opposites which is holy.[26]

This is neatly done symbolically, but it remains quite vague in terms of any social, political, or cultural application; and as Goodheart points out, this is also true of the polarities of *Twilight in Italy*. The two infinites are left in conflict—is there any resolution?

The only resolution, at this point in Lawrence's career, would seem to exist in the nature of the book itself. *Twilight in Italy* develops the dark-light and flesh-spirit polarities that form the basis of speculative works such as the "Study of Thomas Hardy" and "The Crown" and of novels such as *The Rainbow, Women in Love*, and *The Plumed Serpent*. The essays, however, necessarily emphasize the intellectual component in their form and style. The novels express the contrast visually, as in the juxtaposition in the opening paragraph of *The Rainbow* of the horizontal land and the church tower standing above it, or dramatically, as in Birkin's flight in Chapter X of *Women in Love* from the threatening confines of Breadalby to the sensual natural beauty of the surrounding hills. *Twilight in Italy*, however, encompasses both abstract and concrete elements in its execution. As I have shown, the "consummation" or "resolution" of opposites is elusive in *Twilight in Italy*: it cannot be explained in social, political, or historical terms. Stephen J. Miko, writing of the "Study of Thomas Hardy," discusses Lawrence's difficulty in expressing the nature of the reconciliation he seeks. But it is significant that Miko describes the problem as an artistic one, one which is also implicit in Lawrence's novels.

> Lawrence's task as a novelist entails a continual struggle for relation. From the most abstract height this struggle may be viewed as the perennial problem of the One and the Many, but in terms of his writing it amounts to a double commitment to the "primary data" of experience, discrete by nature, along with an equally powerful need to reveal larger wholes by which the divisions implicit in discreteness may be overcome.[27]

In other words, the conflict between world and mind that dominates Lawrence's writing is expressed in its very texture, and it is only in the *style* of a perfectly balanced book like *Twilight in Italy* that the two elements are in any way resolved. For example, in his account of the performance at Gargnano of "una dramma inglese... *Amleto*," Lawrence gives a sensitive, amused, and amusing picture of the production, with its "burly little peasant woman" for queen, "obediently [doing] her best to be important" and its hulking Hamlet, "with his head ducked between his shoulders, pecking and poking, creeping about after other people." This Hamlet, carrying a "black rag of a cloak, something for him to twist about as he twisted in his own soul" becomes for Lawrence an expression of "the modern Italian, suspicious, isolated, self-nauseated, labouring in a sense of physical corruption." This revealing version of Shakespeare's Prince of Denmark leads Lawrence to a contemplation of Shakespeare's historical milieu and the triumph, in the decades that followed Shakespeare's death, of the principle of the not-self, the spiritual infinite. Yet Lawrence's theorizing is held in tension with everyday realities by references to the play being enacted in the Gargnano theatre: "Essere, o non essere, e qui il punto"; and his memory of a performance he saw as a child: "'Amblet, 'Amblet, I *am* thy father's ghost" (*TI*, 119-37; 66-75; 85-97). *Twilight in Italy* characteristically juxtaposes descriptions of immediate experience, serious analyses of that experience, and high and low comedy to create an artistic whole that is an embodiment of the interplay of mind and world.

Evidence that Lawrence conceived of artistic creation in such dualistic terms can be seen as early as his college days. Jessie Chambers has reported the following conversation:

> 'You see, it was really George Eliot who started it all,' Lawrence was saying in the deliberate way he had of speaking when he was trying to work something out in his own mind. 'And how wild they all were with her for doing it. It was she who started putting all the action inside. Before, you know, with Fielding and the others, it had been outside. Now I wonder which is right?'
>
> I always found myself most interested in what people thought and experienced within themselves, so I ventured the opinion that George Eliot was right.
>
> 'I wonder if she was,' Lawrence replied thoughtfully. 'You know I can't help thinking there ought to be a bit of both.'[28]

In 1908, in Eastwood, Lawrence gave a talk on "Art and the Individual" in which he described two schools of esthetic thought that have existed "since the beginning of such thought." The first, which Lawrence identified with Hegel, holds that art is the expression of "the perfect and divine Idea." The second holds that art is a spontaneous activity associated with play, sexuality, emotion, and sensory pleasure.

> In the interpretation we have accepted, these two, the mystical and sensual ideas of Art are blended. Approval of Harmony—that is sensual—approval of Adaptation—that is mystic—of course none of this is rigid.[29]

The two theories of art are clearly related to the polarities that pervade *Twilight in Italy,* and the paragraph quoted above is particularly significant in its insistence upon a coexistence of opposites. The art of Botticelli, as described in *Twilight in Italy* and the "Hardy" study, represents such a balance: "For in Botticelli the dual marriage is perfect, or almost perfect, body and spirit reconciled, or almost reconciled, in a perfect dual consummation."[30] In "The Crown" Lawrence again identifies art as the locus of such consummations.

> Only matter is a very slow flux, the waves ebbing slowly apart. So we engrave the beloved image on the slow, slow, wave. We have the image in marble, or in pictured colour.
>
> This is art, the revelation of a pure, an absolute relation between the two eternities.[31]

There are several images of such consummation in *Twilight in Italy.* The old wool-spinner of Gargnano symbolizes not only the past, but also and more convincingly the immediate moment. Again and again Lawrence emphasizes her spontaneity, which is contrasted with the "before and after" of the monks. Giovanni Fiori, the son of a sensual father and a mother who looks toward the world of ideas, is an embodiment of the dynamic interaction of opposites.

> Giovanni was beautiful, gentle, and courtly like Paolo, but warm, like Maria, ready to flush like a girl with anger or confusion. He stood straight and tall, and seemed to look into the far distance with his clear grey eyes. Yet also he could look at one and touch one with his look, he could meet one. (*TI*, 155-56; 86; 110)

Most importantly there is Lawrence himself at the end of "The Lemon Gardens," contemplating the sensual Italian past and the mechanical English future and finding himself unable to choose between them or between the ways of life they imply. The passage is an almost perfect microcosm of the book's style, for in it Lawrence modulates from a generalized image drawn from his memories of England to a description of the scene immediately before him and then to an abstract statement of one of the book's central themes.

> There was London and the industrial counties spreading like a blackness over all the world, horrible, in the end destructive. And the Garden was so lovely under the sky of sunshine, it was intolerable. For away, beyond all the snowy Alps, with the iridescence of eternal ice above them, was this England, black and foul and dry, with her soul worn down, almost worn away. And England was conquering the world with her machines and her horrible destruction of natural life. She was conquering the whole world.
>   And yet, was she not herself finished in this work? She had had enough. She had conquered the natural life to the end: she was replete with the conquest of the outer world, satisfied with the destruction of the Self. She would cease, she would turn round; or else expire.
>
> (*TI*, 95-96; 53-54; 68-69)

The art of *Twilight in Italy* is the embodiment and vindication of Lawrence's dualistic concept of the two infinites, for it contains in its texture the dark and the light, the body and the spirit, the past and the future, world and mind: the immediate sensual apprehension that is characteristic of Lawrence's poetry and the probing analysis that also found expression in essays like the "Study of Thomas Hardy" and "The Crown." The social and political implications of *Twilight in Italy* are unclear, and Lawrence would continue to try to work them out in his later travel books and other works. For this book only apparently ends in resignation to the triumph of the not-self,

41

the intellect, the machine, and mechanized warfare; it actually brings Lawrence to a crossroads from which he can contemplate his sense of the two paths available to mankind. In *Twilight in Italy* resolution of the two infinites is not found in the politics or the economics or the social behaviors of Europe or the world. Foreshadowing the conclusion to which Lawrence came in *Etruscan Places*, the book suggests that such resolution can be found, perhaps, only in "the clash and foam of the meeting waves": in the individual consciousness at the height of physical and intellectual sensitivity, and in artistic expressions of that consciousness—like *Twilight in Italy* itself.

CHAPTER III

A Diary of Disillusionment

Sea and Sardinia, which appeared in 1921, five years after the publication of *Twilight in Italy,* has received high praise from Lawrence's critics. Anthony Burgess calls it "perhaps the most charming of all the books Lawrence ever wrote"[1] and Keith Aldritt has singled it out as Lawrence's "most unified, sustained, and successful book" of the early twenties.[2] In Aldritt's opinion, "this relaxed and modest undertaking seems perfectly in accord with Lawrence's state of mind in a way that his fictional enterprises of the time do not."[3] It is true that *Sea and Sardinia* makes a strong initial impression, largely because of its vividness of description and the way in which external observation is placed in the context of candid self-portraiture. It gives its readers the impression of a whole man, never a contrived persona, freely recounting his experiences. But narration and description form only one aspect of the book; it also reflects Lawrence's impulse to analyze and prescribe, and in *Sea and Sardinia* this second, more didactic, element is not effectively integrated with the narration and description. Whereas in *Twilight in Italy* the values of mind and world interact in constructive tension, here they are confused and unresolved.

More than the other travel books, *Sea and Sardinia* resembles a diary; in fact, Lawrence's provisional title was *A Diary of a Trip to Sardinia. Twilight in Italy* and *Mornings in Mexico,* as I have suggested, consist of carefully and somewhat artificially organized groupings of episodes. *Sea and Sardinia* gives a running present-tense account of D. H. and Frieda Lawrence's journey from Taormina, Sicily, where they resided at the time, to Sardinia and back in January 1921.[4] It resembles a diary or notebook, as well, in having provided material for other works, particularly poems. The bray of an ass described near the beginning of the first chapter is almost certainly the source of the poem "The Ass" in *Birds, Beasts and Flowers* (*SS,* 18; 5; 5). The Sicilian dawn of the same passage, "The sky and sea . . . parting like an oyster shell, with a low red gape," was to become a symbol of the resurrection of the body in section IX of "The Ship of Death." "Almond Trees," another poem from *Birds, Beasts and Flowers,* may have had its inspiration in the sight of the almond trees near Orosei (*SS,* 274; 157-58; 156-57). Yet *Sea and Sardinia* is not a diary; although it was written quickly, it was written

43

after the Lawrences had returned to Taormina.[5] David Ellis has observed that the apparent immediacy of narrative in *Sea and Sardinia* is the result of "the continual suppression ... of the hindsight available to the man who sits at home and can see his recent journey in perspective."[6] The impression the reader has of following Lawrence day by day and mile by mile has been created through the conscious exercise of literary craft.

Lawrence's letters reveal a curiously ambivalent attitude toward *Sea and Sardinia*. A letter to Scofield Thayer of *The Dial* suggests that the book was written on Thayer's request.[7] When Lawrence sent the manuscript to Curtis Brown, he instructed him to "try and sell this book to periodicals—or part of it. And I don't care how much the editors cut it."[8] Yet in a letter to Earl Brewster dated November 16, 1921, he complained about the "mutilated bits" *The Dial* had published.[9] It may be that in retrospect Lawrence recognized that the book has a unity that was violated by the publication of excerpts. It is a unity that depends on the force of Lawrence's own personality. Both favourable and unfavourable reviewers and critics have remarked on the unusually personal focus of *Sea and Sardinia*. Henry B. Fuller wrote disapprovingly in *The Freeman* that it "exhibits a temperament before a shifting background."[10] David Cavitch agrees, but considers this the book's special recommendation: "The romance and brilliance that the reader enjoys in following this excursion center in the figure of Lawrence alone."[11] Lawrence emerges in *Sea and Sardinia* as the complex man—sensitive, enthusiastic, moody, sometimes irascible—who is recognizable from a reading of the various memoirs and biographies of him. Richard Aldington observes, "In *Sea and Sardinia* there is a quite unconscious portrait of the author, that irresistably charming Lawrence who had the gift of making even the most commonplace things seem wonderful."[12]

Whether the self-portrait was in fact unconscious is debatable, but it seems that here more than anywhere else Lawrence presented himself candidly, with scrupulous honesty. As Cavitch puts it, "in that book he sees a limited, half-comical mortal man—whose attractiveness is only in his subtle awareness of life, including his self-awareness."[13] In *Sea and Sardinia* even more than in *Twilight in Italy* Lawrence displays his strangeness as an Englishman in the Mediterranean—in Richard Mayne's words, "very English, a bit of a fusspot and sometimes rude."[14] He is stereotypically Northern European in his disgust at the dirt of Mediterranean towns. On the voyage of Sardinia he and Frieda decide to debark for a look at Trapani.

> One should not, and we knew it. One should never enter into these southern towns that look so nice, so lovely, from the outside. However, we thought we would buy some cakes. So we crossed the avenue which

looks so beautiful from the sea, and which, when you get into it, is a cross between an outside place where you throw rubbish and a bumpy unmade road in a raw suburb, with a few iron seats, and a litter of old straw and rag. . . . A few mangy, nothing-to-do people stand disconsolately about, in southern fashion, as if they had been left there, waterlogged, by the last flood, and were waiting for the next flood to wash them further.

(SS, 72-73; 37; 37)

At an inn in Sorgono, Lawrence lets his disgust at Sardinian indifference overcome him when he is told that there is no coffee because there is no sugar, and he dresses down the innkeeper.

"Why," say I, lapsing into the Italian rhetorical manner, "why do you keep an inn? Why do you write the word Ristorante so large, when you have nothing to offer people and don't intend to have anything? Why do you have the impudence to take in travellers? What does it mean, that this is an inn. . . ." (SS, 207; 118; 117-18)

Yet while he can be unreasonable, idiosyncratic, and even rude, Lawrence is too sensitive not to realize what kind of impression he must make on others. During a bus ride to Terranova, the point of departure for the steamer back to the mainland, the conductor expresses a deprecating sympathy for his driver, whose obsession with punctuality makes him nervous when passengers and postmen cause a delay.

Never was such a language of sympathy as the Italian. *Poverino! Poverino!* They are never happy unless they are sympathizing pityingly with somebody. And I rather felt that I was thrown in with the *poverini* who had to be pitied for being *nervosi*. Which did not improve my temper.

(SS, 291; 168; 167)

Although Lawrence can sometimes caricature himself, he is irritated when others see him as a caricature—not as an individual but as a representative of his nation. His suffering from the Italian preoccupation with *il cambio*, the rate of exchange, is a leitmotif in *Sea and Sardinia*. On the outward journey the ship's carpenter harangues him about the difficulty the Italians have in buying English coal.

Because why. The price. The exchange! *il cambio.* Now I am doubly in for it. Two countries had been able to keep their money high—England and America. The English Sovereign—la sterlina—and the American dollar—sa, these were money. The English and the Americans flocked to Italy, with their *sterline* and their *dollari*, and they bought what they wanted for nothing, for nothing. Ecco! Whereas we poor Italians—we are in a state of ruination—proper ruination. The Allies, etc. etc.

(SS, 91; 48; 48)

He hears much the same from a schoolmistress and a travelling salesman on the return journey. While he admits that there is some justification for the Italian envy and dislike of England, he resents its effect on how people see him—as a representative of a place on the map.

> We, England, have taken upon ourselves for so long the role of leading nation. And if now, in the war or after the war, we have led them all into a real old swinery—which we have, not withstanding all Entente cant— then they have a legitimate grudge against us. . . .
> And still, for all that, I must insist that I am a single human being, an individual, not a mere national unit, a mere chip of l'Inghilterra or la Germania. I am not a chip off any nasty old block. I am myself.
>
> (SS, 343-44; 198-99; 197-98)

The tendency, explicit in *Twilight in Italy* and sometimes implicit in *Sea and Sardinia*, to theorize about "national character" is here qualified by Lawrence's personal resentment at being seen as he sometimes sees others. This is the special value of the candor Lawrence displays in the travel books, and especially in this one: we see the whole man, revealed in his fascinating complexity. He can generalize about national identity, the "races," but when he is his everyday self—here a rather hurt and angry self—his fundamental insistence on the uniqueness of the individual shines through. The fascinating thing is that neither Lawrence is a pose. The theoretician who generalizes about national character and the hurt human being are one man.

The honesty of Lawrence's self-portrait is also apparent in the way he reacts to the things he sees and the people he meets. Although he depicts himself as being ready to romanticize, he never does so for long; yet he finds and acknowledges beauty wherever it is—beauty that others usually overlook. In the middle of grumbling about the dirtiness of the port of Palermo and the smallness of his ship, he suddenly notices its fittings.

> Those maplewood panels and ebony curves—and those Hygeias! They went all round, even round the curve at the dim distant end, and back up the near side. Yet how lovely beautiful old gold-coloured maplewood is! how very lovely, with the ebony curves of the door arch! There was a wonderful old-fashioned Victorian glow in it, and a certain splendour.
>
> (SS, 47; 22; 22)

In the miserable inn at Sorgono, Lawrence is lifted out of his "black, black, black" rage by the sight of the open fire, "like new gold," and an old man roasting a goat before it. Lawrence recognizes the wisdom of the Italian proverb which says that "Man can live without food, but he can't live without fire," and he is filled with admiration at the old man's absorption in his task.

He held the candle and looked for a long time at the sizzling side of the meat, as if he would read portents. Then he held his spit to the fire again. And it was as if time immemorial were toasting itself another meal. I sat holding the candle. (*SS*, 182; 102-03; 102)

The candor of *Sea and Sardinia* is perhaps best exemplified in Lawrence's account of his reactions to a religious procession and service in the little village of Tonara. He describes the costumes of the villagers in beautiful, loving detail, but when he sees beside the altar the "modern, simpering, black-gowned Anthony of Padua" and hears the unctuous and barren voice of the priest delivering a simple-minded sermon he is reminded that the procession was, after all, just another manifestation of "this dreary Christianity of ours" (*SS*, 224; 128; 127). Yet when he realizes that the parishioners are being distracted by the presence of two foreigners in the doorway he tells Frieda, "Come away . . . Come away, and let them listen." And he concludes, "it was a wonderful place."

Usually, the life-level is reckoned at sea level. But here, in the heart of Sardinia, the life-level is high as the golden-lit plateau, and the sea-level is somewhere far away, below, in the gloom, it does not signify. The life-level is high up, high and sun-sweetened and among rocks.
(*SS*, 224-25; 128; 128)

When Lawrence's responses to a place are based on fantasy he is willing to admit it. Nearing Orosei, one of the last stops before Terranova and the steamer, he remarks on the magnificence of its setting. Orosei is beautiful from a distance, and though it proves a "dilapidated, sun-smitten, godforsaken little town" he is willing to romanticize over it for a moment—and then to acknowledge its reality.

Oh, wonderful Orosei, with your almonds and your reedy river, throbbing, throbbing with light and the sea's nearness, and all so lost, in a world long gone by, lingering as legends linger on. It is hard to believe that it is real. It seems so long since life left it and memory transfigured it into pure glamour, lost away like a lost pearl on the east Sardinian coast. Yet there it is, with a few grumpy inhabitants who won't even give you a crust of bread. And probably there is malaria—almost sure. And it would be hell to have to live there for a month. Yet for a moment, that January morning, how wonderful, oh, the timeless glamour of those Middle Ages when men were lordly and violent and shadowed with death.
(*SS*, 275; 158; 157)

This is the characteristic tone, or rather an example of the characteristic modulation of tone, of *Sea and Sardinia*. Lawrence gives us, spontaneously and directly, what he sees and what it means to him, moving from romantic rapture to bold description to waspish criticism and back again, all in a few sentences.

Although as I have demonstrated *Sea and Sardinia* resembles a diary and is most successful in that sense, it is not merely a record of places and people and Lawrence's immediate reactions to them. It is built upon two not wholly compatible themes: the Sardinia journey as a search for an austere, purposeful "masculine" society, and as a flight from the sterile modernity of mainland Europe. Cavitch has identified the "plot" which he believes underlies the book: "Lawrence hankers after spontaneous passional adventure as a respite from the self-awareness that is sometimes like a madness."[15] This hankering can be understood more clearly in terms of the contrast between the "masculine" and "feminine" modes of consciousness to which Lawrence gives exposition in the "Study of Thomas Hardy" and *Fantasia of the Unconscious*. In the Hardy study he maintains, not very originally or very convincingly, that "man, the male, is essentially a thing of movement and time and change"; he is governed by the "Will-to-Motion." Woman, on the other hand, he identifies with the "Will-to-Inertia," a "feeling of Immutability, Permanence, Eternality."[16] In the Hardy study and in most of Lawrence's writing, the great goal is to reconcile or to maintain a creative tension between these two forces, which are expressions of what I have identified as mind and world. In *Fantasia of the Unconscious* and in *Sea and Sardinia*, the goal is the freeing of the masculine Will-to-Motion from the feminine Will-to-Inertia, so that man may act purposefully in the temporal sphere. In *Fantasia of the Unconscious* Lawrence sees man as having, since the Renaissance, entered the female mode: "Now, his consummation is in feeling, not in action," and this, he believes, is wrong. "Of course the woman should stick to her own natural emotional positivity. But then man must stick to his own positivity of *being*, of action, of *disinterested, non-domestic*, male action, which is not devoted to increase of the female."[17] Lawrence's concept of this impulse to action was behind his explanation in *Twilight in Italy* of why so many Italian men wanted to leave their villages for America.

> It is not the money. It is the profound desire to rehabilitate themselves, to recover some dignity as men, as producers, as workers, as creators from the spirit, not only from the flesh. It is a profound desire to get away from women altogether, the terrible subjugation to sex, the phallic worship.
>
> (*TI*, 104-05; 59; 75)

A similar impulse seems to have been at least partially responsible for Lawrence's interest during the War in giving a series of joint lectures with Bertrand Russell. Lawrence was convinced that a social revolution would be inevitable in England after the War, and he was eager to take a role in shaping it. Lawrence's lectures were never given, but the following passage from a letter to Russell suggests the lines they might have followed.

> I have only to stick to my vision of a life when men are freer from the immediate material things, where they need never be as they are now on the defense against each other, largely because of the struggle for existence, which is a real thing, even to those who need not make the struggle. So a vision of a better life must include a revolution of society. And one must fulfill one's vision as much as possible. And the drama shall be between individual men and women, not between nations and classes. And the great living experience for every man is his adventure into the woman. And the ultimate passion of every man is to be within himself the whole of mankind—which I call social passion—which is what brings fruit to your philosophical writings. The man embraces in the woman all that is not himself, and from that one resultant, from that embrace, comes every new action.[18]

Paradoxically, what Lawrence later labelled "male" action in the social sphere was to be taken for the purpose of giving man the freedom from economic pressure that would enable him to "adventure into the woman" in order to embrace "all that is not himself." In this letter Lawrence unconsciously reveals the ambivalence of his attitude towards social action. He saw the need for change on a large scale, and he was looking for a way to bring it about; but the goal of the revolution he envisioned was the fulfillment of the individual through sexual-religious experience. Perhaps he was groping toward an expression on a societal level of the reconciliation of the polarities of female and male and self and not-self that he had defined symbolically in *Twilight in Italy*. Though it was written six years after this letter, Lawrence's second travel book reflects a similar pattern of thought.

In *Sea and Sardinia* the feminine principle is identified, as Cavitch observes,[19] with Mt. Etna, the "wicked witch" that dominates the Sicilian landscape.

> Ah, what a mistress, this Etna! with her strange winds prowling round her like Circe's panthers, some black, some white. With her strange, remote communications and her terrible dynamic exhalations. She makes men mad. Such terrible vibrations of wicked and beautiful electricity she throws about her, like a deadly net!   (*SS*, 13; 2; 2)

Etna becomes the symbol for the feminine Will-to-Inertia from which Lawrence feels he must escape: "Perhaps it is she one must flee from" (*SS*, 14; 3; 3). Thus Lawrence conceives the Sardinian trip as an essentially masculine enterprise; he fantasizes about a more perfect form the journey might take.

49

To find three masculine, world-lost souls, and, world-lost, saunter and saunter on along with them, across the dithering space, as long as life lasts! Why come to anchor? There is nothing to anchor for. Land has no answer to the soul anymore. It has gone inert. Give me a little ship, kind gods, and three world-lost comrades.   (SS, 87; 46; 46)

Ironically, Lawrence sets out not with three world-lost comrades but with Frieda, the q-b, the queen-bee—his anchor, his land, his Etna—another representative, for him, of the Will-to-Inertia. Oblivious to the paradox, Lawrence repeatedly calls his readers' attention to Sardinian manifestations of what Edward Nehls calls "the fierce maleness that was slowly dying out in the course of Western Civilization."[20] Nehls has quoted from the following passage, but I reproduce it here because it summarizes the qualities Lawrence found so appealing in the men of Sardinia.

I see my first peasant in costume. He is an elderly, upright, handsome man, beautiful in the black-and-white costume. . . . How handsome he is, and so beautifully male! . . . How fascinating it is, after the soft Italians, to see these limbs in their close knee-breeches, so definite, so manly, with the old fierceness in them still. One realises, with horror, that the race of men is almost extinct in Europe. Only Christ-like heroes and woman-worshipping Don Juans, and rabid equality-mongrels. The old, hardy, indomitable male is gone. His fierce singleness is quenched. The last sparks are dying out in Sardinia and Spain.   (SS, 113-14; 61-62; 61-62)

Lawrence remarks on the "*essential* courtesy" and the "sensitive, manly simplicity" of the Sardinian patrons of the Inn at Tonara: "They knew that in the beginning and in the end, a man stands alone, his soul is alone in itself, and all attributes are nothing—and this curious final knowledge preserved them in simplicity" (SS, 235; 134; 134). The independence, the essential aloneness in the self, of the Sardinian men impresses Lawrence and becomes for him evidence that there are individuals who have not given in to the sameness of the increasingly cosmopolitan world and its universal consciousness. He remarks of a group of workers in the train to Sorgono,

It is wonderful in them that at this time of day they still wear their long stocking caps as a part of their inevitable selves. It is a sign of obstinate and powerful tenacity. They are not going to be broken in upon by world-consciousness. They are not going into the world's common clothes.
(SS, 162; 91; 90)
I love my indomitable coarse men from mountain Sardinia, for their stocking-caps and their splendid, animal-like stupidity. If only the last wave of all-alikeness won't wash those superb crests, those caps, away.
(SS, 164-65; 92; 92)

In their "splendid, animal-like stupidity" these Sardinians are, like the wool-spinner of *Twilight in Italy*, representatives of the sensual, pre-conscious past. Their individualism, pure, inborn, and unselfconscious, seems a powerful antidote to the "mob-spirit" which Lawrence felt had seized men during the War, undermining their potential for integrity and wholeness, that he would later describe in the "Nightmare" chapter of *Kangaroo*.

> It was the whole spirit of the war, the vast mob-spirit, which [Somers] could never acquiesce in. The terrible, terrible war made so fearful because in every country practically every man lost his head, and lost his own manly isolation in his own integrity, which alone keeps life real. Practically every man being caught away from himself, as in some horrible flood, and swept away with the ghastly masses of other men, utterly unable to speak, or feel for himself, or to stand on his own feet, delivered over and swirling in the current, suffocated for the time being. Some of them to die for ever. Most to come home victorious in circumstance, but with their inner pride gone: inwardly lost.[21]

In *Sea and Sardinia* Lawrence sees two possibilities for the future of civilization after the War: a world characterized by "grey proletarian homogeneity" (the outcome of a triumph of socialism or communism), or one in which "we are going to swing back into more-or-less isolated, separate, defiant communities" (*SS*, 163, 91, 91). He favours the latter, and imagines these Sardinians to be precursors of a reaction against "world-assimilation and world-oneness" which he believed was being manifested also in growing isolationism in Russia and America, and which he was to attribute to the Diggers of *Kangaroo* and the Men of Quetzalcoatl in *The Plumed Serpent*. The "last sparks" of "fierce singleness' may be dying out, but Lawrence values them and holds out a hope that they might be revived. Lawrence's projection of these qualities that he finds so admirable in a small group of Sardinian workmen upon a larger scale, however, points up some of the shortcomings of his political thinking. It is difficult to imagine how "separate, defiant communities," unless they were far more isolated than is in fact possible in the modern world, could avoid becoming embroiled in struggles which, like the First World War, would make it virtually impossible for men to retain their individual integrity.

As S. Ronald Weiner has suggested in his article on *Sea and Sardinia*, the book describes a journey that was both geographically and thematically circular.[22] The final pages give an account of a marionette performance in Palermo. The performance was of the story of the Paladins of France, who fight and defeat the Knights of Spain, a dragon, and a great old witch. Weiner comments:

[The witch] and her "smoke and sulphur" servant [Beelzebub] are, in short, a recapitulation of Etna, which was earlier described as Circe the enchanting witch. She is defeated, though not finally destroyed, by a union of Merlin's intelligence and the "surging hot" blood-power of the Paladins. The knights in their armor, who are isolate individuals, but one company leagued together against mental corruption, become a gently ironic symbol of the Sardinians. The eager knight of Britain, who specializes in words rather than deeds and who falsely claims to have slain the foe, seems almost a parodic reference to Lawrence himself, who through the words of his book is attempting a similar conquest.[23]

Evidence to support the idea that the marionette performance may be interpreted as a recapitulation of the desire for a freeing of the male principle of action from the female Will-to-Inertia is abundant. Lawrence comments approvingly that except for Frieda the audience is limited to males, "urchins or men," and the mood of the performance is strictly masculine. "Again the old male Adam began to stir at the roots of my soul. Again the old, first-hand indifference, the rich, untamed male blood rocked down my veins" (*SS*, 351; 203; 202). The old witch has a "horrible, girning female soul which locks up the heroes, and which sends forth the awful and almost omnipotent malevolence." Lawrence sees in her the "white, submerged idea of woman which rules from the deeps of the unconscious" (*SS*, 353; 204; 203).

The pattern that governs *Sea and Sardinia* when it is read in these terms is typical of what Lawrence was writing during this period. Philip Rieff writes in his introduction to the Viking edition of Lawrence's books on the unconscious, "For both Lawrence and Freud, women distract men from the missions in the world upon which they must embark. The feminine is the specifically anti-cultural force. Alone, or in a company of like-minded men, the husband must set out from his home to make something new and better in the world."[24] That this is a change from the conceptual system that governed the works of the period of *Twilight in Italy* and the Hardy study can be seen when one recognizes that in the earlier works the male and female principles, the "two infinites," are considered to be equally necessary to the achievement of wholeness. In *Fantasia of the Unconscious* and by implication in *Sea and Sardinia* the two are seen as being separable, and the male principle is considered the greater. Lawrence's quarrel with Freud is over what he calls the psychiatrist's insistence that "a sexual motive can be attributed to all human activity." Lawrence maintains that there is "something else, of even higher importance. . . ."

And what is this other, greater impulse? It is the desire of the human male to build a world: not "to build for you, dear," but to build up out of his own self and his own belief and his own effort something wonder-ful.[25]

As in the Hardy study, man is the thinker and doer ("mind"), and woman is the initiator of emotion and sympathetic understanding ("world").[26] But now the two work not in concert but in opposition. The confusion of symbolic meanings in *Sea and Sardinia* is exemplified by the fact that the marionette witch is identified with intellection, whereas elsewhere the female principle is identified with the sensual ground of being, the life-awareness that Lawrence now attributes admiringly to the *men* of Sardinia. F. von Broembsen's distinction between primal individuality and modern self-assertive individualism[27] is relevant here. Lawrence recognizes in the Sardinian males the primitive self-sufficiency (a "feminine" quality) that he had seen in the woolspinner of Gargnano, but he takes them also as an inspiration for positive "masculine" action in the contemporary context. They exhibit qualities that belong to the "feminine" side of the polarity that Lawrence had outlined in the "Study of Thomas Hardy," yet they are identified with the Paladins who go forth to battle the witch. In other words, Lawrence celebrates their unconscious self-integration but also tries to make them models for conscious emulation. It was not until after Lawrence's exposure to the American Indians and to the relics of Etruscan culture that he distinguished clearly between primitive selfhood and the conscious striving of modern political man.

Beyond this as yet unresolved inconsistency, the pattern of *Sea and Sardinia* foreshadows the plots of Lawrence's "leadership" novels: Aaron Sisson's flight from his wife and family into the masculine society dominated by Rawdon Lilly, Richard Lovat Somers' search for masculine friendship in the context of political action, and Don Ramón Carrasco's creation of a revolutionary brotherhood in which connection to the female is seen as necessary but definitely subordinate. Indeed, Don Ramón and Don Cipriano in *The Plumed Serpent* can be seen as extensions of the "fiercely male" Sardinian peasants Lawrence so admired. In these terms *Sea and Sardinia* marks the beginning of Lawrence's temporary deflection from his basic belief in creative interaction between the masculine Will-to-Motion and the feminine Will-to-Inertia, the two infinites of not-self and self, the impulses of mind and world. Significantly, the novels of the early twenties are almost universally considered Lawrence's least successful. In them Lawrence underplays the need for balance between the male and female principles that had governed his earlier—and would govern his later—works, and insists upon the independence of the man in his effort to "build a world." As Padraic Colum observed in his review of *Sea and Sardinia*, "in life it is different."[28] The marionette castle is still dominated by the witch; the feminine principle cannot be ignored. In his later works Lawrence was to regain the perspective that acknowledged the importance of the two infinites to a truly meaningful way of life.

I have suggested that there is a second underlying theme in *Sea and Sardinia* which is not quite compatible with that of the search for a field for masculine action; it is the desire to find an alternative to the sterile intellectualism of modern Europe (in other words, an alternative to the qualities which in his "Study of Thomas Hardy" Lawrence had labelled "masculine"). In this sense *Sea and Sardinia* can be seen as a continuation of *Twilight in Italy* and a further movement along the curve of return that leads to *Mornings in Mexico* and *Etruscan Places*: a flight from civilization, "the horror of human tension, the absolute insanity and machine persistence" (*SS*, 54; 26; 26), toward a more valid old—and potentially new—world. In *Twilight in Italy* northern Europe is the locus of the mental-spiritual principle, Italy of the physical principle, the "Original, Creative Infinite." By the time he wrote *Sea and Sardinia*, however, Lawrence could no longer look to Italy as a source of spontaneous vitality. Perhaps he felt that the War had so accelerated the modernization of attitudes and environment that he had already noted in 1913 that Italy was now virtually indistinguishable from the North in its absorption in the machine; or perhaps by 1921 Italy simply seemed too familiar. In any case, Lawrence felt that the Italian land had "become humanised, through and through: and we in our own tissued consciousness bear the results of this humanisation. . . . And then—and then —there is a final feeling of sterility. It is all worked out. It is all known: *connu, connu!*" (*SS*, 215-16; 123; 122). Now Lawrence looks to Sardinia as a source of freshness and of a new sensual awakening. It is one of the "unknown, unworked lands where the salt has not lost its savour" (*SS*, 216; 123; 123). He chooses to travel to Sardinia because "it lies outside; outside the circuit of civilisation" (*SS*, 15; 3; 3).

The landscape surrounding Cagliari, as Lawrence first views it, seems to belong to nowhere: "Land and sea both seem to give out, exhausted at the bay head: the world's end." Here, surely, is a place where mental consciousness can be left behind.

> The spirit of the place is a strange thing. Our mechanical age tries to override it. But it does not succeed. In the end the strange, sinister spirit of the place, so diverse and adverse in differing places, will smash our mechanical oneness into smithereens, and all that we think the real thing will go off with a pop, and we shall be left staring. (*SS*, 103; 55; 55)

In contrast to the "romantic-classic," "eighteenth century" landscape of Italy, which seems to have been finished by the hand of a humanistic artist, Sardinia is wild and open.

> This gives a sense of space, which is so lacking in Italy. Lovely space about one, and travelling distances—nothing finished, nothing final. It is like liberty itself, after the peaky confinement of Sicily. Room—give me room—give me room for my spirit: and you can have all the toppling crags of romance. (*SS*, 131; 72; 72)

Similarly, Lawrence contrasts the people of Cagliari, "warm and good-natured, like human beings," with the "non-human ancient-souled Sicilians, who are suave and so completely callous" (*SS*, 101; 54; 54). He believes he sees in Sardinian eyes "a stranger, older note: before the soul became self-conscious: before the mentality of Greece appeared in the world. Remote, always remote, as if the intelligence lay deep within the cave, and never came forward" (*SS*, 123; 67; 67). In a passage deleted in typescript, Lawrence noted approvingly that unlike the Italians, the Sardinians do not think abstractly. For them "mankind" does not exist; there are only individuals.[29] Lawrence is captivated by the vitality displayed by the maskers at Nuoro, "the good old energy of the bygone days, before men became so self-conscious" (*SS*, 250; 144; 143), and by the reluctance of the men to return seriously to work on the Monday after a festival, which "shows a spark of spirit, still holding out against our over-harnessed world" (*SS*, 261; 150; 149). As earlier among the people at San Gaudenzio and later among the American Indians, Lawrence seeks and at least for a time seems to find among the Sardinians a living alternative to the self-consciousness and frenzy of the modern world.

But to sustain such a view of Sardinia and its people Lawrence would have had to close his eyes to much of what he encountered. If in Sardinia he was seeking a civilization exempt from the stresses of modern life, a society in which a kind of primitive goodness and ingenuousness could flourish, he returned disillusioned. Several weeks after the excursion he wrote to Rosalind Popham, "We went to Sardinia—it was an exciting little trip—but one couldn't live there—one would be weary—dreary. I was very disappointed."[30] The chapter "To Sorgono" can be interpreted as an emblem of Lawrence's disillusionment. He and Frieda set off in a train with great anticipation: "Sorgono we feel will be lovely" (*SS*, 153; 85; 85). At first it seems so.

> But we are almost there—look, look, Sorgono, nestling beautifully among the wooded slopes in front. Oh, magic little town. Ah, you terminus and ganglion of the inland roads, we hope in you for a pleasant inn and happy company. (*SS*, 169; 94-95; 94)

But the lone inn is filthy, the innkeeper sullen and indifferent, the only places for a stroll the stony high-road—a "dreary hole" with no shops, a "weary-looking church, and a clutch of disconsolate houses"—and a side-lane that serves as the outdoor public lavatory. The countryside is beautiful, but Lawrence is too furious to enjoy it. In less than an hour he is eager to leave "the Sodom apple of this vile village" as soon as he can—at half-past seven the next morning (*SS*, 172-74; 96-98; 96-97). Frieda chides him for his unreasonable anger, counselling him to "take it as it comes. . . . It's all life."

> But no, my rage is black, black, black. Why, heaven knows. But I think it was because Sorgono has seemed so fascinating to me, when I imagined it beforehand. Oh, so fascinating! If I had expected nothing I should not have been so hit. Blessed is he that expecteth nothing, for he shall not be disappointed.
> I cursed the degenerate aborigines, the dirty-breasted host who *dared* to keep such an inn, the sordid villagers who had the baseness to squat their beastly human nastiness in this upland valley. (*SS*, 176-77; 99; 99)

Lawrence's outrage then, has its source not so much in the reality of Sorgono as in its failure to fulfill his imagination of it. The setting is Edenic, but the savages are far from noble. Instead of a place for a new beginning Lawrence finds only hopeless squalor.

In Sardinia as in Italy Lawrence encountered a manifestation of the desire, contradicting his own, to escape from primitive surroundings to the modern world of the North. The bus conductor who engages the Lawrences in conversation on the last leg of their overland journey asks leading questions about conditions in England and America, and finally reveals his obsession: "'*Andare fuori dell' Italia.*' To go out of Italy. To go out—away—to go away—to go away. It has become a craving, a neurasthenia with them" (*SS*, 280; 161; 160). The bus conductor has a home on the coast, and nearby he owns land. "But he doesn't want to work it. He doesn't want it. He hates the land, he detests looking after vines. He can't even bring himself to try any more" (*SS*, 281; 162; 161). He wants to emigrate to England or America and become a chauffeur. Like John in the "San Gaudenzio" section of *Twilight in Italy* he feels stifled in the simple surroundings Lawrence would like to believe might foster an alternative to modern society. John and the bus conductor are not as far along in the historical life-development; they have emerged from the state of the primitive too recently to recognize, as Lawrence eventually did, the importance of the curve of return to the success of a journey into the future.

56

The final passage of *Sea and Sardinia* is elegiac in tone. Lawrence has travelled in search of a place where the elemental relationship of man with his environment might be regained, and he has been disappointed. As much as he admires the warmth of some of the Sardinians and the gentle innocence of his fellow theatre-goers in Palermo, he cannot be at one with them.

> All is over. The theatre empties in a moment. And I shake hands with my fat neighbour, affectionately, and in the right spirit. Truly I loved them all in the theatre: the generous, hot southern blood, so subtle and spontaneous, that asks for blood contact, not for mental communion or spirit sympathy. I was sorry to leave them. (*SS*, 355; 205; 204)

And yet he must, for he cannot be one of them.

The excellence of *Sea and Sardinia* lies in the honesty and vitality of Lawrence's re-creation of what he saw, in Sardinia and in himself, in the course of the journey. But the book reveals a conflict within Lawrence between the forces of world and mind that was temporarily debilitating rather than constructive. He sought in Sardinia on the one hand a manifestation of the simple sensual life that was already dying out in Italy, and on the other hand an embodiment of the "masculine" will to action that might be put to work rebuilding Western society on a model of fierce independence; he found neither consistently and convincingly. Sardinia put Lawrence's discontent with modern civilization in a new light, and on one level it set the pattern for the "leadership" novels of the early twenties. But Lawrence's disillusionment with the reality of Sardinia and his disappointment at its failure to provide a consistently satisfying example of a society of "fierce maleness" foreshadowed the inconclusiveness of *Aaron's Rod*, *Kangaroo*, and *The Plumed Serpent*. Lawrence's desire, following the impulse of the prophetic mind, to bend the world to a preconceived ideal had been defeated in Sardinia, yet he apparently felt compelled to write it out in fiction. It was only in New Mexico that Lawrence found an actual living culture that seemed to be based on the principles he cherished, and that discovery was to force him to realize that those principles could not, after all, be put directly into action in the contemporary world.

CHAPTER IV

The Spark of Contact

Lawrence once wrote that New Mexico had given him what was probably his "greatest experience from the outside," one that changed him forever by liberating him "from the present era of civilisation, the great era of material and mechanistic development."[1] That experience was, Lawrence explained, a religious one: "I had no permanent feeling of religion till I came to New Mexico and penetrated into the old human race-experience there. It is curious that it should be America, of all places, that a European should get a sense of living religion from the Red Indians, having failed to get it from Hindus or Sicilian Catholics or Cingalese."[2] Or perhaps it is not so curious, after all. In *The Lost Girl*, published in 1920 (nearly two years before Lawrence first visited America), Alvina Houghton, a middle-class Midlands girl, is irresistibly drawn to Ciccio, a young Italian member of troupe of music hall "Indians"; Ciccio embodies the dark forces of intuition that Lawrence later emphasized in his descriptions of American Indians. In the letter to Earl Brewster in which Lawrence related Mabel Dodge Sterne's invitation to come to her ranch at Taos, New Mexico, he admitted, "The Indian, the Aztec, Old Mexico—all that fascinates me and has fascinated me for years. *There* is glamour and magic for me."[3] Lawrence seems to have been quite ready to have a significant experience in New Mexico. How that experience *changed* him, however, is not immediately obvious. *The Plumed Serpent*, the best-known literary product of Lawrence's time in America, seems an extension, albeit one greatly influenced by its setting, of the concerns and ideas that were implicit in the novels *Aaron's Rod* and especially *Kangaroo*: an interest in social action and a belief in the natural election of certain individuals to lead the mass of men. *Mornings in Mexico*, on the surface, seems to continue Lawrence's survey of relatively "primitive" societies and his search for a culture that would promote the creation of a more nearly perfect mode of living through the reconciliation or at least the fruitful interaction of the "two infinites." But a careful consideration of this third of Lawrence's travel books suggests that his experiences in New Mexico did indeed change his understanding of the relationship between civilization and pre-civilization and with it the character of his own quest for meaning in life.

The Lawrences received Mabel Sterne's invitation on November 5, 1921, and arrived at Taos on September 11 of the following year—having travelled from Taormina via Ceylon, Australia, and briefly, Tahiti. Lawrence's first impressions of New Mexico were mixed, at best. Writing to S. S. Koteliansky on September 18, he related how upon his arrival Mabel immediately sent him "motoring off to an Apache gathering 120 miles away across desert and through cañons.... Mabel Sterne ... wants me to *write* this country up. God knows if I shall."[4] He found the Apaches "not very sympatisch," and he soon began to feel the constraints of "living under the wing of the 'padrona.'"[5] It was not until Lawrence had put some distance between himself and Mabel, first by moving, in December of 1922, to Del Monte Ranch at Questa, some seventeen miles from Taos, and then by spending several months in Mexico in 1923, that he was able to begin to confront America on his own terms. The first draft of the novel *The Plumed Serpent* was written in Chapala, Mexico, in the summer of 1923, and the first of the essays that were collected in *Mornings in Mexico* were apparently written in the spring and summer of 1924 after the Lawrences, having been reunited in England after a separation of three months, had returned to Taos.[6] These are the essays dealing with the Indians of New Mexico. The essays describing Oaxaca, which precede the New Mexican essays in the book, date from December 1924,[7] and the final chapter ("A Little Moonshine With Lemon") was apparently written in Spotorno, Italy, on St. Catherine's Day, November 25, 1925. The essays appeared in various magazines between July 1924 and February 1927, and *Mornings in Mexico* was published in June 1927 by Martin Secker.[8]

As he does in his other travel books, Lawrence reveals himself quite directly in *Mornings in Mexico*, and again the revelation is dual: we see Lawrence the traveler, the recorder of impressions of his surroundings, and also Lawrence the thinker, whose experiences inform the development of his philosophy. The book opens with a passage that seeks to minimize the scope implied in the title: "One says Mexico: one means, after all, one little town away South in the Republic...." That is, the subject is a small portion of the world, as it is encountered first-hand. "All it amounts to is one little individual looking at a bit of sky and trees, then looking down at the page of his exercise book" (*MM*, 9; 1). The first, Oaxacan, section of the book moves gradually outward from this focus, to the dog and the parrots that inhabit the patio in which Lawrence writes, to the people of a nearby village, and finally to the larger community that forms in Oaxaca on market day; and with that movement comes a broadening of philosophical perspective. Lawrence's subject is not, it turns out, just one sleepy little town but the Mexican and Indian ways of life and their implications for Western man.

59

Yet the by now familiar figure of Lawrence the traveler remains at the center. The exasperation of the Englishman at a dirty Sardinian inn is echoed in his frustration in trying to buy a few oranges in the little village of Huyapa. He goes from store to store and house to house, and is finally directed to the house where he began his search.

> The lounging man was peeping out of the gateless gateway, as we came, at us.
> "It is the same place!" cried Rosalino [Lawrence's servant], with a laugh of bashful agony.
> But we don't belong to the ruling race for nothing. Into the yard we march. (*MM*, 46; 19)

In *Twilight in Italy* and particularly in *Sea and Sardinia* Lawrence's narrative is sometimes at odds with the book's theoretical aspect. Here, direct observations lead more clearly to generalizations: mind and world are not so obviously in tension. In the opening chapter, Lawrence's description of the distance between the innocent behaviour of the dog Corasmin and the implied mockery of the parrots' imitations of him are the basis of his theoretical observations about the unbridgeable distances between man and non-human creation and between "modern" and "primitive" men. Similarly, on market day Lawrence barters briefly for a pair of sandals, breaking off the negotiations by saying with a grimace that they smell. His retrospective comment moves from the incident itself to historical observations, and finally to a realization of the difference between the Mexican and European perceptions of things.

> They did [stink]. The natives use human excrement for tanning leather. When Bernal Diaz came with Cortez to the great marketplace of Mexico City, in Montezuma's day, he saw the little pots of human excrement in rows for sale, and the leathermakers going around sniffing to see which was the best, before they paid for it. It staggered even a fifteenth-century Spaniard. Yet my leather man and his wife think it screamingly funny that I smell the huaraches before buying them. Everything has its own smell, and the natural smell of huaraches is what it is. (*MM*, 89-90; 41)

The texture of *Mornings in Mexico* is more even than that of earlier travel books; the modulations between internal and external narration and theoretical exposition, between seriousness and irony and self-deprecation, are more subtle. Some of what Lawrence writes about the Pueblo deer dance applies to the style of *Mornings in Mexico*.

> Everything is very soft, subtle, delicate. There is none of the hardness of representation. They are not representing something, not even playing. It is a soft, subtle, *being* something.

Yet at the same time it is a game. . . . And all eyes are round with wonder, and the mystery of participation. Amused, too, on the merely human
side of themselves. The gay touch of amusement in buffoonery does not in
the least detract from the delicate, pulsing wonder of solemnity, which
comes from participating in the ceremony itself.   (*MM*, 110-11; 50)

Mornings in Mexico is full of amusement and self-amusement, and also of
wonder; and it is, as I shall demonstrate, a kind of ceremony of self-awak-
ening.

Underlying *Mornings in Mexico* is the same polarity of civilization and
the primitive that was developed in the earlier travel books. It is manifested
most obviously in Lawrence's description of the contrast between the idle
curiosity of the tourists who come to witness the Hopi snake dance and the
solemnity of the Indians who perform it.

People trail hundreds of miles, avidly, to see this circus-performance of
men handling live rattlesnakes that may bite them any minute—even do
bite them. Some show, that!

*   *   *

Before the snake dance begins, on the Monday, and the spectators are
packed thick on the ground round the square, and in the window-holes,
and on all the roofs, all sorts of people greedy with curiosity, a little speech
is made to them all, asking the audience to be silent and respectful, as this
is a sacred religious ceremonial of the Hopi Indians, and not a public
entertainment. Therefore, please, no clapping or cheering or applause, but
remember you are, as it were, in a church.
    The audience accepts the implied rebuke in good faith, and looks round
with a grin at the 'church'. But it is a good-humoured, very decent crowd,
ready to respect any sort of feelings. And the Indian with his 'religion' is a
sort of public pet.   (*MM*, 138-39; 63)

But the contrast between the Indian-Mexican and Western world-views goes
far deeper. In the middle of his account of the snake dance Lawrence observes,

We have undertaken the scientific conquest of forces, of natural conditions. It has been comparatively easy, and we are victors. . . .
    The Hopi sought the conquest by means of mystic, living will that is in
man, pitted against the living will of dragon-cosmos. The Egyptians long
ago made a partial conquest by other means. Our corn doesn't fail us: we
have no seven years' famine, and apparently need never have. But the
other thing fails us, the strange inward sun of life. . . .   (*MM*, 145-46; 67)

Describing the Mexican landscape, Lawrence observes that everything seems
"to be slowly wheeling and pivoting upon a centre" (*MM*, 80; 36). The

market of Oaxaca seems a vortex possessed of a centripetal force, drawing the people of the region to it and then sending them out again, in a regular rhythm. Lawrence finds it strange, in this setting, that Western man "should think in straight lines, when there are none, and talk of straight courses, when every course, sooner or later, is seen to be making the sweep round, swooping upon the centre. . . . The straight course is hacked out in wounds, against the will of the world" (*MM*, 80-81; 36). The primitive life acknowledges and reflects the cylical nature of things: the turning of earth on its axis in its orbit around the sun, the eternal round of birth, procreation, death, decay and new life. Modern Western man has imposed a linear course on this cyclical pattern: headlong progress toward a fixed goal, expressed in the end-stopped process of manufacture, use, and disposal. It is in their acquiescence to and participation in the eternal natural cycles that primitive men, according to Lawrence, come to touch with a cosmic power that eludes us.

As I have already observed, Lawrence wrote that his American experience gave him his first "sense of living religion." The difference between the Indian religious experience and the Western concept of religion is suggested in the tourists' amused reaction to the admonition that the square in which the snake dance takes place and the landscape that surrounds it constitute a kind of church. For modern Western man, religion (if it has any significance at all) is one increasingly subordinate aspect of a compartmentalized life. He occasionally goes to a building, constructed for the purpose, to worship a transcendent God. In contrast, "The American aborigines are radically, innately religious. The fabric of their life is religion. But their religion is animistic, their sources are dark and impersonal, their conflict with their 'gods' is slow, and unceasing" (*MM*, 167-68; 79). Lawrence knew a good deal about animism from his reading of Edward Taylor's *Primitive Culture*,[9] but his contact with the American Indians gave him a profound understanding of its pervasiveness in the primitive experience of the world.

> There is strictly no god. The Indian does not consider himself as created, and therefore external to God, or the creature of God. To the Indian there is no conception of a defined God. Creation is in great floods forever flowing, in lovely and terrible waves. In everything, the shimmer of creation, and never the finality of the created. Never the distinction between God and God's creation, or between Spirit and Matter. Everything, everything is the wonderful shimmer of creation. . . . (*MM*, 112-13; 51)

No distinction between spirit and matter! It should not be surprising that Lawrence, who for years had been wrestling with that very distinction which is so ingrained in the Western consciousness, should write that New Mexico changed him forever. Indeed, the vision of life that Lawrence projects in his description of the animism of the American Indians underlies all of his later important works, from *Etruscan Places* to *Last Poems*. Its central concept is the vitality of the cosmos, the aliveness of all things.

> In the oldest religion, everything was alive, not supernaturally but naturally alive. There were only deeper and deeper streams of life, vibrations of life more and more vast. . . . The whole life-effort of a man was to get his life into direct contact with the elemental life of the cosmos. . . . To come into immediate *felt* contact, and so derive energy, power, and a dark sort of joy.[10]

Dexter Martin, discussing *Mornings in Mexico* from an anthropological perspective, attests that Lawrence had understood, or felt, the spirit of Indian religion with amazing accuracy: "Lawrence goes deeper than the anthropologists who try to sum up Pueblo religion as animism or nature worship. . . . Lawrence gives us something very important: a sense of the richness and warmth of [an animistic] world."[11] An anthropologist, of course, studies a culture objectively, with scientific detachment. If Lawrence's understanding of Indian religion was so keen, it was because it awakened sympathetic echoes in his own mind and heart.

Lawrence found in the religion of the American Indians a cultural expression of the philosophy of "blood-knowledge" and the importance of immediate apprehension of experience that he had begun to develop many years before.[12] Lawrence calls Indian song "an experience of the human bloodstream, not of the mind or spirit" (*MM*, 105; 47). William York Tindall has observed that Lawrence's response to the Indian songs and dances had apparently been conditioned by his reading of Frazer's *The Golden Bough*, Tylor's *Primitive Culture*, Jane Harrison's *Ancient Art and Ritual*, and the writings of Madame Blavatsky;[13] one must add Frederick Carter's *The Dragon of the Alchemists*, which Lawrence read in manuscript during his stay at Chapala in 1923.[14] From Mme. Blavatsky Lawrence took the idea, which he expressed in the Foreword to his *Fantasia of the Unconscious*, that there was a time during the glacial period in which cultures all over the world were in contact and shared the "science" that we recognize today as astrology. After the melting of the glaciers some peoples degenerated into cave-men, while some, "like Druids or Etruscans or Chaldeans or Amerindians or Chinese, refused to forget, but taught the old wisdom, only in its half-forgotten, symbolic forms."[15] Lawrence found some evidence in support of this idea in Zelia Nuttall's *The Fundamental Principles of Old and New World Religions*[16] and in W. H. Prescott's *History of the Conquest of Mexico*,[17] both of which he read in 1923. In "The Hopi Snake Dance" Lawrence drew on his reading of Frederick Carter to describe the nature of the Indian's relation to the cosmos, linking it with the ancient religions of the Eastern hemisphere.

> We must remember, to the animistic vision there is no perfect God behind us, who created us from his knowledge, and fore-ordained all things. No such God. Behind lies only the terrific, terrible crude source, the mystic Sun, the well-head of all things. From this mystic Sun emanate the Dragons, Rain, Wind, Thunder, Shine, Light. The Potencies or Powers. (*MM*, 143; 65-66)

It is interesting to note that in the manuscript of this chapter there are no references to "dragons"; Lawrence added this symbolic touch in the process of revision.[18] The dragon images here and in related passages seem to owe less to the ubiquitous plumed serpents of Old Mexico than to Frederick Carter. In *The Dragon of Revelation*, an expansion of the book which Lawrence saw in manuscript in Chapala, Carter explains that the importance of dragons in primitive mythologies stems from the polar position of Draco in the circle of the Zodiac. According to Carter "the dragon naturally was called the first created being by the Chaldean theologers . . . to him are due all those irregularities in heaven and vagaries in time coming from the erring planets, all that which causes defect in man's judgement and sets him at odds with his years and his days. . . . He is the maker of eclipses, the disturber of regularity and order. Yet is it not he by and through whom man gains admittance to the topmost heaven?"[19] Lawrence adopted the dragon image, making it a symbol of primitive man's constant need to conquer the powers of the cosmos—not through science but "by means of the living will" striving against the wills of the dragons. In the animistic view, religion is not a matter of the supplication of deities, but of continual self-creation in the matrix of the living universe (*MM*, 143-44; 66).

The preceding might seem to imply that in *Mornings in Mexico*—particularly in the New Mexican chapters—Lawrence was describing an ideal community of spontaneous primitives with which he could identify and in which he might somehow participate. But the book's relation to Lawrence's dream of such a community (his Rananim) is more complex. Coming face to face at last with real aboriginals, not Italian peasants or Sardinian herdsmen, Lawrence drew back—not in a moment of reaction against the unfamiliar but more decisively and permanently. There is, to be sure, a certain superficial reserve reflected in Lawrence's initial characterization of the Apaches as "not very sympatisch." And a kind of sarcasm dominates the letter to Willard Johnson which he wrote immediately after seeing the Hopi snake dance[20]—though a comparison of that letter with the account of the dance published in *Mornings in Mexico* demonstrates that Lawrence's sympathy with and understanding of Indian ceremony soon grew and deepened. But Lawrence's ultimate reaction against a personal acceptance of the Indian way of life had more profound sources.

As early as *Twilight in Italy* Lawrence had recognized that, like the *padrone* and Il Duro, he could not turn his back on the modern world and embrace the past wholeheartedly. In his Introduction to Maurice Magnus' *Memoirs of the Foreign Legion*, published in 1924 but recounting events of 1919 and 1920, Lawrence described talking with Magnus, who was then living at the monastery of Monte Cassino south of Rome, "on a wild hill-top high above the world":

> This was the mountain top, the last foothold of the old world. Below we could see the plain, the straight white road, straight as a thought, and the more flexible black railway with the railway station. There swarmed the ferrovieri like ants. There was democracy, industrialism, socialism, the red flag of the communists and the red, white and green tricolor of the fascisti. That was another world. And how bitter, how barren a world! Barren like the black cinder-track of the railway, with its two steel lines.
> And here above, sitting with the little stretch of pale, dry thistles around us, our back to a warm rock, we were in the Middle Ages. Both worlds were agony to me. But here, on the mountain top was worst: the past, the poignancy of the not-quite-dead past.
> "I think one's got to go through with the life down there—get somewhere beyond it. One can't go back," I told him.[21]

Lawrence expressed a similar perception with regard to the South Sea Islanders in his essay on Melville's *Typee* and *Omoo*. In its simplicity and in the directness of its confrontation with natural forces the primitive life is undeniably attractive, but "one cannot go back."

> Some men can: renegade. But Melville couldn't go back: and I now know that I could never go back. Back towards the past, savage life. One cannot go back. It is one's destiny inside one.
> There are these peoples, these "savages." One does not despise them. One does not feel superior. But there is a gulf in time and being. I cannot commingle my being with theirs.[22]

A sense of a similar gulf between Lawrence and the Mexican peasants and the New Mexican Indians runs throughout *Mornings in Mexico*. Ronald P. Draper notes Lawrence's "profound sympathy with the world of the primitive poetic imagination," but adds that "the Indian way of consciousness cannot be connected with ours; nor does Lawrence in the last resort want to surrender his European consciousness."[23] But Lawrence's distance from the Indian experience was not a matter of a desire to retain his European identity; it was an expression of the deep gulf he saw between the Indian and himself. This is stated most explicitly and colorfully, perhaps, in his essay "Indians and an Englishman." He describes the "voice out of a far-off time" of an old Apache who is speaking and chanting before the firelight:

> It was not for me, and I knew it. Nor had I any curiosity to understand. . . . Our darkest tissues are twisted in this old tribal experience, our warmest blood came out of the old tribal fire. And they still vibrate in answer, our blood, our tissue. But me, the conscious me, I have gone a long road since then. . . . I don't want to go back to them, ah, never. I never want to deny them or break with them. But there is no going back. Always onward, still further. The great devious onward-flowing stream of conscious human blood. From them to me, and from me on.
>
> *   *   *
>
> . . . I stand on the far edge of their firelight, and am neither denied nor accepted. My way is my own, old red father; I can't cluster at the drum any more.[24]

That the radical discontinuity between the modern and the primitive experiences of the world is the central theme of *Mornings in Mexico* has been convincingly demonstrated by Thomas R. Whitaker.[25] Whitaker points out that the theme is introduced when in the first chapter, "Corasmin and the Parrots," Lawrence reflects on the parrots' mockery of him, his servant Rosalino, and the little dog Corasmin: the parrots imitate jeeringly, Lawrence claims, because they recognize that they have been superseded by higher life-forms. In his whimsical analysis of the "conversation" that takes place in his courtyard, Lawrence rejects the idea of evolution: he asserts that each life-form (parrot, dog, or man, for example) is so different from the others that it must have arisen spontaneously. Each life-form inhabits a different order of existence.

> Myself, I don't believe in evolution, like a long string hooked on to a First Cause, and being slowly twisted in unbroken continuity through the ages. I prefer to believe in what the Aztecs called Suns: that is, Worlds successively created and destroyed. The sun itself convulses, and the worlds go out like so many candles when somebody coughs in the middle of them. Then subtly, mysteriously, the sun convulses again, and a new set of worlds begins to flicker alight. (*MM*, 15; 4)

Each life-form exists in a different dimension, totally separate from the others.[26] Even Lawrence the modern European and Rosalino the primitive Mexican live in different dimensions, under different "Suns." "Between us also is the gulf of the other dimension, and he wants to bridge it with the foot-rule of three-dimensional space. He knows it can't be done. So do I. Each of us knows the other knows" (*MM*, 22-23; 8). An animal cannot reach to man, and a sensual, primitive man like Rosalino cannot reach across to the world of the modern Western consciousness. Whitaker sees in the three succeeding chapters a gradual movement toward a limited, momentary transcendence of this mutual isolation. In "Walk to Huayapa" Lawrence and Rosalino are given unripe fruit by an old woman, and since she refuses payment they give her their empty lemonade bottle, which to her is "a treasure." Whitaker observes, "Each party in this brief meeting, so charged with silent communication, receives his reward, and pride begins to yield to delight and mutual respect."[27] "The Mozo," a portrait of Rosalino, extends and deepens this sense of communication and understanding. Lawrence recognizes that Rosalino as an Indian cannot comprehend his own European insistence on the importance of exactitude in the computation of time, distance, and money, just as he had at first been baffled by Rosalino's indifference to such values. But as he learns more about Rosalino, Lawrence recognizes a common bond. Like Lawrence, Rosalino was a draft resister, a man with a "horror of serving in a mass of men" (*MM*, 74; 33). Whitaker sees the final chapter about Old Mexico, "Market Day," which, significantly, has been moved from its original position among the essays to become the last of the series,[28] as a culmination of Lawrence's movement toward an accommodation with his alien surroundings. The market is a place of meeting, and market day is a ritual the real purpose of which is not commerce but human contact—contact with others different from oneself.

> And here [the people coming to market] have felt life concentrate upon them, they have been jammed between the soft hot bodies of strange men come from afar, they have heard the sound of strangers' voices in their ears, they have asked and had been answered in unaccustomed ways.
>
> (*MM*, 91-92; 42)

They meet each other, and Lawrence meets them, in an intangible, fleeting moment, "forever gone, forever coming, never to be detained: the spark of contact" (*MM*, 92; 42).

But the moment of contact is brief. The New Mexican essays return forcefully to the evocation of an unbridgeable gulf between the modern and the primitive modes of consciousness. "Indians and Entertainment" begins by contrasting the Western idea of entertainment, involving a drama and spectators, with the Indians' sense of participation. The audience of a Western drama is like a disembodied "watchful spirit," detached from the action on the stage. For the Indian "there is no division between actor and audience. It is all one."

67

The Indian is completely embedded in the wonder of his own drama. It is a drama that has no beginning and no end, it is all-inclusive. It can't be judged, because there is nothing outside it, to judge it.

$$(MM, 115; 53)$$

This contrast is a corollary of the fundamental difference between the modern and the primitive views of the universe. Modern Western man looks on the rest of the world as being separate from himself. He examines it, studies it, and constructs abstractions—history, science—to "explain" it. Primitive man confronts the world as a whole, from the inside. Instead of analyzing it, he participates in it. Lawrence insists that the difference is so basic as to be irreconcilable.

The Indian way of consciousness is different from and fatal to our way of consciousness. Our way of consciousness is different from and fatal to the Indian. The two ways, the two streams, are never to be united. They are not even to be reconciled. There is no bridge, no canal of connection.

$$(MM, 102; 45-46)$$

Lawrence adds that we make a serious mistake when we try to pretend that all humanity is one stream. And "to pretend to express one stream in terms of another, so as to identify the two, is false and sentimental" (MM, 103; 46). This is the real source of paradox in the Hopis' solemn announcement to the tourists that they must behave during the snake dance as if they were in a church. The analogy is so weak as to be humorous, because the context and character of the Hopi ceremony are so radically different from those of Christian worship.

Lawrence follows his own warnings in "The Dance of the Sprouting Corn" and "The Hopi Snake Dance." These chapters are not attempts to convince Western readers of the validity or preferability of the Indian way, nor are they attempts to explain the Indian ceremonies by comparing them with Western religious observances. Rather, they seek to evoke, inevitably from the outside, the nature and significance of the Indian way, the way of participation in the wonder of the earth's cycles. In his description of the corn dance Lawrence emphasizes the downward plunge of the dance, "towards the earth's red centre, where these men belong" (MM, 127; 58); the snake dance is a part of the Hopi's confrontation with the "mysterious life-spirit" that reigns in the New Mexican mesas: "The eagle and the snake" (MM, 145; 67). And Lawrence ends "The Hopi Snake Dance" with a reiteration of the distance between the modern and primitive ways.

Soon after the dance is over, the Navajo begin to ride down the Western trail, into the light.... We say they look wild. But they have the remoteness of their religion, their animistic vision, in their eyes, they can't see as we see. And they cannot accept us. They stare at us as the coyotes stare at us: the gulf of mutual negation between us. (*MM*, 168-69; 79)

In accounts of Lawrence's work between 1920, when he took up residence in Taormina, and 1926, when he settled near Florence to write *Lady Chatterley's Lover*, emphasis has generally been placed on his novels—*Aaron's Rod*, *Kangaroo*, and especially *The Plumed Serpent*—making this Lawrence's "leadership period," characterized by a devaluation of the individual and an attraction to the modern idea of community and to authoritarian political structures.[29] For example, Baruch Hochman asserts that after World War I "Lawrence no longer lays massive emphasis on the resources of individual men ... the goal of individual effort changes, as does the individual's relation to community."[30] Scott Sanders puts this shift in emphasis in religious terms:

> ... Lawrence shifted from a Protestant to a Catholic view of the relation between man and God. In the early works every man was his own priest, apprehending the movements of the creative impulse within himself; but in the works written in the decade that followed 1915, it appears that the priests must intercede between the common man and God, for only the elect can discover and embody the divine will. In the works subsequent to 1925 ... Lawrence reverted to his earlier position.[31]

The "elect" Sanders has in mind would include Birkin, Lilly, Kangaroo, and especially Don Ramón Carrasco. He invokes Catholicism in his attempt to characterize Lawrence's socio-political views during this "middle period" partly because of the analogy between the Catholic reliance on hierarchy and Lawrence's belief in an "organic" social structure depending on benevolent rule by a natural aristocracy (a kind of primitive Toryism without the Tories), but also because Lawrence's conception of the function of society *was* essentially religious.

> So, the new system will be established upon the living religious faculty in men. In some men this faculty has a more direct expression in consciousness than in other men. Some men are aware of the deep troublings of the creative sources of their own souls.... In other men the troublings are dumb, they will never come forth in expression, unless they find a mediator, a minister, an interpreter.[32]

Lawrence insisted, in *The Plumed Serpent* and in various essays on this period, that only a few exceptional individuals have the innate capacity to understand fully and interpret correctly the laws of God—or the cosmos—to man, and that they therefore should not only function as spiritual intermediaries, but should by a kind of divine right be temporal rulers as well.[33]

Lawrence's ideas about the possibility of the reformation of society through the advent of a natural aristocracy may have been based in part on his own ascent from the working class to a position of prominence, but they also bear a striking resemblance to some of the social theories of Thomas Carlyle and John Ruskin, with whose writings Lawrence was familiar by his middle twenties.[34] The young Carlyle, like Lawrence almost a century later, found himself in a society which had replaced the old feudal "organic" connection between master and worker with industrialism, *laissez-faire* economics, and the "cash nexus," a society which he believed was therefore teetering on the brink of a revolution that would replace the rule of unworthy leaders with the rule of an equally unworthy mob. Carlyle's answer was in the development of a new kind of leadership, a "truer and truer *Aristocracy*, or government again by the *Best*."[35] Such leadership could only be found, according to Carlyle, by a people worthy of it, a people who had re-created themselves spiritually. Frederick William Roe's summary of Carlyle's notion of how such a spiritual restoration might be fostered shows how closely Lawrence echoed Carlyle's ideas.

> To the logical, calculating, scientific, severely rationalistic temper, [Carlyle] opposed the mystical, spontaneous, poetic, and imaginative temper. He pleaded for a renewal in man of his ancestral wonder in the common things of life, since the truly supernatural is forever the natural. . . . Most of all, like a prophet of Israel he called upon his contemporaries to re-enthrone righteousness and justice in their hearts as the source of every energy which could permanently recreate the world in which they lived.[36]

Lawrence's views on leadership have been compared to Nietzsche's, but their connection to Carlyle's is more direct. The Victorian essayist advised, "Find in any country the Ablest man who exists there; raise *him* to the supreme place, and loyally reverence him: you have a perfect government for that country."[37] For Carlyle, as later for Lawrence, wisdom and an innate sense of justice, not merely the ability to use force effectively, were the marks of a true leader.

Like Carlyle, whom he revered, John Ruskin believed in hierarchy and aristocracy, but not in the pleasure-loving hereditary aristocracy or the new aristocracy of wealthy industrialists. His ideal, like Carlyle's (and like Lawrence's) was essentially feudal: he believed that workers for whom work had been made fulfilling (by the elimination, insofar as possible, of demeaning machine-tending and a return to the more personally rewarding hand-labour of earlier times) would be content to leave larger questions to just governors. Like Carlyle, Ruskin believed that "all effectual advancement toward [the] true felicity of the human race must be by individual effort,"[38] and that through such effort men could become capable of choosing the best among them as their rulers. Even Lawrence's dream of Rananim may have owed something to Ruskin's example. In 1871 Ruskin set about establishing the Guild of St. George, which he hoped would found a series of communities engaged in agriculture and handicrafts and run on paternalistic, feudal principles. Ruskin's project advanced further than Lawrence's—centres were actually established in Wales, Worcestershire, and Yorkshire—but it ultimately failed for lack of sufficient financial support.[39] At any rate, Lawrence shared with and quite possibly borrowed from Carlyle and Ruskin the idea of a "better" society that would be hierarchically structured and founded on the rightness of spirit of its members.

The type of leadership that Lawrence's Don Ramón seeks to provide has a religious foundation, but it has secular political overtones as well, and Lawrence has frequently been criticized for flirting with fascism in *The Plumed Serpent*. In this regard it is instructive to compare two letters Lawrence wrote on October 9, 1925: to Martin Secker he declared, "I *do* mean what Ramón means—for all of us"; to Carl Seelig he observed, "I don't like politics at all—don't believe in them."[40] In the novel Don Ramón repeatedly asserts that his movement to revive the worship of the ancient Mexican deities is not fundamentally political. Responding to Don Cipriano's suggestion that he seek the Presidency, he states, "I must stand in another world, and act in another world.—Politics must go their own way, and society must do it as well."[41] Still, Don Ramón's movement does develop along political lines, and its violent excesses clearly point up, for the book's readers if not for Lawrence himself, the extreme danger of following Ramón's philosophy to its logical conclusion in the sphere of political action. Yet *Mornings in Mexico*, written during the time when Lawrence was working on *The Plumed Serpent* and from the same materials, qualifies the impression of Lawrence's thought in the early nineteen-twenties that the novel alone would create. If in the fiction of *The Plumed Serpent* Lawrence gave free play to the systematizing impulse of mind, in the non-fiction travel book he admitted the moderating impulse of world. As David Cavitch has observed, the Oaxaca essays reveal Lawrence "feeling sheepish as an author, perhaps already embarrassed by what he was driven to write in his Mexican novel.... There was that grace of irony in Lawrence that could anticipate his repudiation of the overblown fantasy he was writing even while his emotional self had to pursue it to the end."[42] Scott Sanders has commented that through Kate Leslie, Lawrence introduces into *The Plumed Serpent* something of the "balanced, ambivalent" response to the "savage mysteries" that is reflected in *Studies in Classic American Literature, Mornings in Mexico*, and the essays on New Mexico which were collected in *Phoenix*.[43] Mark Schorer sees Lawrence in his leadership period seeking "escapes from freedom,"[44] but this is not strictly true even of *The Plumed Serpent*, where, as L. D. Clark has observed, for Don Ramón "the hope of mankind lies not in the system but in the individual conscience."[45] It is even less true of *Mornings in Mexico*, in which the emphasis, in spite of Lawrence's evocations of primitive community, is on the individual and on the concept of "otherness" that he had developed in the poems of *Look! We Have Come Through!* and *Birds, Beasts and Flowers*.

In the first chapter of *Mornings in Mexico* Lawrence establishes the idea that each order of beings lives under a different "sun," in a separate "dimension." The poem "Fish" also expresses this idea; of a fish he has caught and holds, still alive, in his hands, Lawrence writes: "*. . . I am not the measure of creation. / This is beyond me, this fish. / His God stands outside my God.*"[46] In "Corasmin and the Parrots," as I have noted, Lawrence maintains that even his servant Rosalino inhabits an alien dimension. The essay "Democracy" (1919) had applied this perception of otherness to the relations among all individuals, not just classes of men: "The fact that an actual man present before us in an inscrutable and incarnate Mystery, untranslatable, this is the fact upon which any great scheme of social life must be based. It is the fact of otherness."[47] Here again Lawrence echoes Ruskin, who insisted that there were differences "eternal and irreconcilable, between one individual and another, born under absolutely the same circumstances."[48] Lawrence's statement is more mystical in tone, but its import and its political implications are the same. This idea was one of the bases of Lawrence's rejection of Anglo-American democracy, which he believed ignored the fact of otherness, levelling all to the lowest common denominator. It was not in itself a prescription for fascism, but a call for the recognition of radical individuality.

> One man is neither equal nor unequal to another man. When I stand in the presence of another man, and I am my own pure self, am I aware of the presence of an equal, or of an inferior, or of a superior? I am not. When I stand with another man, who is himself, and when I am truly myself, then I am only aware of a Presence, and of the strange reality of Otherness.[49]

The "pure self" is not the striving, self-conscious individual who has been idealized by Western Civilization; he is the person whose selfhood is so innate and natural that it never comes into question. As I have shown, Lawrence believed that the wool-spinner of Gargnano and the Sardinian workmen possess such radical selfhood. Lawrence enlarges on the distinction in his essay, "The Individual Consciousness v. the Social Consciousness":

The moment the human being becomes conscious of himself, he ceases to be himself. The reason is obvious. The moment any individual creature becomes aware of its own individual isolation, it becomes instantaneously aware of that which is outside itself, and forms its limitation. That is, the psyche splits in two, into subjective and objective reality....

*   *   *

Paradoxical as it may sound, the individual is only truly himself when he is unconscious of his own individuality, when he is unaware of his own isolation, when he is not split into subjective and objective, when there is no *me or you*, no *me or it* in his consciousness, but the *me and you*, the *me and it* is a living continuum, as if all were connected by a living membrane.[50]

For Lawrence the "innocent or radical individual consciousness" is "the queer nuclear spark in the protoplasm, which is life itself, in its individual manifestation." When it is lost or denied either through selfishness, "when the 'me' wants to swallow the 'you'" (as in fascism), or through self-abnegation, "when the 'I' wants to lapse out into the 'you' or the 'it'" (as in Western democracy), the result is the death of the self.[51] It is important to recognize that the "true individual" is defined not by his place in a social hierarchy, but by his place in the cosmic continuum. The New Mexican Indians' apparent preservation of "true individualism" was what attracted Lawrence to them, and it was their sense of continuity with the cosmos that he attempted to project, albeit rather clumsily, in *The Plumed Serpent*. The "fascism" of *The Plumed Serpent* is superficial, a matter of uniforms and raised-fist salutes. Don Ramón is concerned with power, but not with temporal power. The Epilogue to Lawrence's textbook *Movements in European History*, which he completed in September 1924,[52] clarifies the distinction: Lawrence differentiates "bullying"—forcing one's will on others—the "worship of mere Force," which he identifies with fascism and Soviet communism, from *power*. Force is irresponsible; power brings profound responsibility.[53] And power is not gained through usurpation or through democratic elections; it is inborn. "There *is* a natural nobility, given by God or the Unknown, and far beyond common sense. And towards this natural nobility we must live."[54] Don Ramón explains to Kate Leslie, "Quetzalcoatl is to me only the symbol of the best a man may be, in the next days."[55] He tells his followers, "We will be masters among men, and lords among men. But lords of men, and masters of men we will not be."[56] It is this kind of power, not the power of one man over another but the power derived from confrontation with the cosmos, that Lawrence believed he saw revealed in the Indian dances of *Mornings in Mexico*. They express the "glory in power of the man of single existence. The peril of the man whose heart is suspended, like a single red star, in a great and complex universe" (*MM*, 108-09; 49). According to Lawrence the Indian's one great commandment is "*Thou shalt acknowledge the wonder*" (*MM*, 116; 53).

> And virtue? Virtue lies in the heroic response to the creative wonder, the utmost response. In the man, it is a valiant putting forth of all his strength to meet and run forward with the wonder. In woman it is the putting forth of all herself in a delicate, marvellous sensitiveness, which draws forth the wonder to herself, and draws the man to the wonder in her.... (*MM*, 116; 53-54)

In his essay "Pan in America" (1924) Lawrence insists that rightly understood, "life itself consists of a live relatedness between man and his universe: sun, moon, stars, earth, trees, flowers, birds, animals, men, everything—and not in a conquest of anything by anything."[57] It is *this* that Lawrence means —"for all of us"—not the overlay of politics, which distorts the core of positive significance in *The Plumed Serpent* and has led critics to misapprehend the effect of Lawrence's American experience on his thought.

The rituals of *The Plumed Serpent* and the descriptions of Mexican life and Indian ceremony in *Mornings in Mexico* are not intended as guides to the conduct of life, for Lawrence himself or for his readers. The movement Lawrence calls for is not into the past, but on a curve of return back *toward* the communal primitive, as a source of renewal for the journey into a new future. As H. M. Daleski has recognized, "Lawrence believes that primitive intuitions may well serve as a point of fresh departure in the onward movement of our civilization; the direction to be taken, however, is forward, not backward, and if this means going back in order to go forward, it is by way of adding something to our lives, not reducing them."[58] To slough off Western culture like a skin and adopt primitive ways would be reduction, retreat, and self-destruction. In *Women in Love* Birkin observes of an African sculpture in Halliday's flat that it represents the ultimate expression of a culture: "It is so sensual as to be final, supreme."[59] For Lawrence anything final is dead. For a modern man to immerse himself in a culture that has already reached its ultimate expression would be to embrace death. In a letter to Else Jaffe written just after his arrival in Taos, Lawrence observed that the American Indians, like civilized Western men, were "up against a dead wall." But, Lawrence insists, we *can* learn from them: we "can go back and pick up some threads" and go ahead on our own.[60] This idea is, as I have observed, echoed in Lawrence's essay on Melville's *Typee and Omoo*: "... as I say, we must make a great swerve in our onward-going life-course now, to gather up again the savage mysteries. But this does not mean going back on ourselves."[61] Throughout *Mornings in Mexico* Lawrence insists on the separateness of the Indian and Western cultures. They exist in two different dimensions, or in the imagery of the Melville essay, they consist of two roads which long ago diverged forever: "through the many centuries since Egypt, we have been living and struggling forward along some road that is no road, and yet it is a great life-development . . . and on we must still go."[62] Yet from the primitive cultures we can gain a new perspective that may enrich and revalidate our own "life-development":

> We can never recover an old vision, once it has been supplanted. But what we can do is to recover a new vision in harmony with the memories of old, far-off, far, far-off experience that lie within us.[63]

The development of Western culture has been toward rationality and mechanical order, away from intuitive, sensual connection with the cosmos; "let us try to adjust ourselves to the Indian outlook," Lawrence suggests, "to take up an old dark thread from their vision, and see again as they see, without forgetting we are ourselves."[64] This would be a way of bringing about the fruitful interaction of "masculine" intellect and action—represented by modern society—and "feminine" physicality and emotion—now represented by primitive cultures. Lawrence calls for a "welling up of religious sources that have been shut down in us," so that our religion would reflect our whole selves and inform every aspect of our lives, bringing "church and house and shop together."[65] As always in Lawrence, the goal expressed in *Mornings in Mexico* and the other essays of the period is balance: not a rejection of mind but a balance of intellect and intuition, the spirit and the senses, mind and world.

Lawrence makes the Oaxacan market day a symbol of this pattern of return, renewal, and onward movement. As the villagers come to the market for revitalization, so, Lawrence believes, must modern man come into touch, however briefly, with primitive life-awareness.

> There is no goal, and no abiding place, and nothing is fixed, not even the cathedral towers. The cathedral towers are slowly leaning, seeking the curve of return. As the natives curved in a strong swirl, towards the vortex of the market. Then on a strong swerve of repulsion, curved out and away again, into space.
> Nothing but the touch, the spark of contact. That, no more. That, which is most elusive, still the only treasure. Come, and gone, and yet the clue itself. (*MM*, 92; 42)

The spark of contact is another expression for the "evening star," Don Ramón's metaphor in *The Plumed Serpent* for the fulfilling illumination that appears at the meeting point of day and night, light and dark, the male and female, reason and intuition—what in the "Study of Thomas Hardy" Lawrence had called the "Holy Ghost." The Mexicans come to the market for a moment of communal contact and then return to their isolated lives, but they have been revitalized by the sound of strange voices and unaccustomed answers. This is the significance of the experiences described in *Mornings in Mexico*. In America Lawrence discovered that there is no Rananim, or at least that it is not to be found outside oneself. Among the Indians Lawrence found the life of spontaneity and cosmic connection that he had thought he was seeking, but he also recognized that it was a life beyond which he had already passed. He was drawn along a curve that had led him through rural Italy and Sardinia to the vortex of community and the primitive animistic apprehension of the cosmos in New Mexico, but he was carried inevitably on a swerve of repulsion beyond it. He couldn't cluster at the drum, and he re-emerged to continue his own journey. In the essay "Democracy," Lawrence wrote, "The great lesson is to learn to break all fixed ideals, to allow the soul's own deep desires to come direct, spontaneous into consciousness. But it is a lesson which will take many aeons to learn."[66] *Mornings in Mexico* represents not the learning of that lesson, the reaching of that goal, but the evanescent spark of contact which provided energy for Lawrence's further journey—to the demanding freedom of the individual seeking to make a life not in the past but in the future.

The geographical and thematic journey described in *Sea and Sardinia* is circular; that of *Mornings in Mexico* is, appropriately, a curve. In the Oaxacan essays Lawrence begins as a European in an exotic land, bemused by the strangeness of his surroundings. Through "Market Day" he moves toward intimate contact with those surroundings and toward a momentary sense of connection with the primitive communal and yet radically individual life-experience that he describes in the New Mexican chapters. The final chapter, "A Little Moonshine With Lemon," finds him back in civilization, alone again. The centrality of individual experience that had been announced at the book's opening in Lawrence's qualification of the pretentiousness of his title is reflected in the self-directed irony of this chapter's epigraph: "Ye Gods, he doth bestride the narrow world like a Colossus . . . !" (*MM*, 173; 80). Lawrence sits alone above the Mediterranean, wondering how his Italian servant Giovanni would react to a call for his favourite bedtime drink of his New Mexican evenings: "*Un poco di char' di luna, con canella e limone.* . . ." But it's impossible; the words are untranslatable. The gulf between the two worlds appears again. The movement of the final chapter is away from Mexico, on the great curve of return to a life-experience not completed, not developed like that of Mexico and New Mexico to a dead end. To Lawrence, who has found a measure of personal renewal in his contact with the communal primitive, the Old World now seems the appropriate place for growth.

> The Mediterranean, so eternally young, the very symbol of youth! And Italy, so reputedly old, yet forever so child-like and naive! Never, never for a moment able to comprehend the wonderful, hoary age of America, the continent of the afterwards. (*MM*, 175-76; 81)

Writing of *Lady Chatterley's Lover*, James C. Cowan has observed that Lawrence came to realize "that the redeeming qualities of the dark consciousness, which aboriginal America embodied for him, are not to be projected outward in the form of grandiose schemes for world regeneration but integrated in the individuation of consciousness within the self."[67] The curve of return described in *Mornings in Mexico* was to lead Lawrence onward to the Etruscans and to the vision of personal and social regeneration, reflected in *Etruscan Places*, *Lady Chatterley's Lover*, and the other works of Lawrence's final years, for which they opened the way.

CHAPTER V

The Mystery of Touch

At the beginning of January 1926, Lawrence included in a letter to John Middleton Murry a bit of New Year's stock-taking: "I'm forty, and I want to enjoy my life. Saying my say and seeing other people sup it up doesn't amount to a hill o' beans, as far as I go. I want to waste no time over it. That's why I have an agent. I want my own life to live."[1] This profession of indifference was soon to be belied by Lawrence's vigorous reaction to the suppressions of *Lady Chatterley's Lover* and *Pansies* and the police confiscation of several of his paintings, but it did reflect a significant change in the subjects and emphases of his writing. *Etruscan Places*, Lawrence's final travel essays, along with *Lady Chatterley's Lover* and the other works of Lawrence's last years, continued the evolution in the focus of his work that had been suggested in *Mornings in Mexico*: a shift away from the sense of immediate social mission and the interest in contemporary politics that had been evident in *Kangaroo* and *The Plumed Serpent*, and toward the more personal vision of human affairs that is centered in the "mystery of touch."

It was among the artifacts of the Etruscans, a mysterious people who flourished between the Tiber and the Arno from the 11th to the 3rd Century B.C., that Lawrence found a focus for the world-view that dominated his writings in the last four years of his life. Lawrence's interest in the Etruscans dated at least from 1921, when he wrote to Catherine Carswell asking for more informatiton about the "secret" which she had seen "written so plainly" in their remains.[2] That interest lay dormant until 1926, when he mentioned to Curtis Brown the possibility of doing "a book, half travel, half study, on Umbria and the Etruscans."[3] Later the same month Lawrence invited Richard Aldington to join him on a walking tour of Tuscany and Umbria, but by the time his plans took shape a year later Earl Brewster had been enlisted as his companion. Between April 6 and 11, 1927, Lawrence and Brewster visited Cerveteri, Tarquinia, Vulci, and Volterra, and by the 9th of June Lawrence could write to Brewster that he had begun his essays.[4]

Four of Lawrence's Etruscan pieces appeared in the American magazine *Travel* between November 1927 and February 1928. The texts of the articles differ slightly from those of the corresponding sections of *Etruscan Places*, but the variations are the result of editorial cuts probably made for reasons of space and propriety. *Etruscan Places* itself, which was published as a book in 1932 and consists of six chapters, is in a sense unfinished. In October 1927, Lawrence wrote to Alfred A. Knopf, whom he hoped to interest in the essays, "I intended to do twelve sketches, on different places—but when I was ill, I left off at Volterra. I wanted to do a book about 80,000 words, with some 80 or 100 photographs."[5] However, Lawrence admitted in this letter to not caring very much whether he finished the project as he had originally conceived it. The book as it was published after Lawrence's death does, in fact, have the formal coherence of a finished work. The opening "Cerveteri" chapter includes what serves as a general introduction, and the sixth chapter ends with an anecdote that (as I will demonstrate) parabolically reflects the book's central theme. Christopher Hassall is correct in observing that "on the plane where archaeological facts may be found to serve a symbolic purpose, the book was complete."[6] Lawrence wrote a seventh chapter, "The Florence Museum," which survives in the autograph manuscript of *Etruscan Places* at the Humanities Research Center of the University of Texas. It is less a description of the museum than a coda to the chapters describing the various Etruscan sites, and it was not offered, like earlier chapters, for periodical publication.

As in his earlier travel books, Lawrence was less interested in providing a practical guidebook than in recording his direct observations to create a symbolic structure. Perhaps because the society he describes in *Etruscan Places* is represented only by fragments—architectural remains, tomb paintings, and artifacts housed in museums—Lawrence's immediate personal response to Etruria is not a reaction so much as a creation, and thus is identical with his intellectual, theoretical response; mind and world are reconciled. In *Twilight in Italy* Lawrence recounted his confrontation with a society in transition from a sensual orientation to a rational one, and the book's texture reflects the conflict between those orientations in that Lawrence both directly described what he saw and analyzed it according to the theoretical system he was developing; the two modes of expression exist in *Twilight in Italy* in a creatitve tension. To Sardinia and Mexico Lawrence brought with him a set of expectations derived from *Twilight in Italy* and the patterns of thought he had articulated in related works such as the "Study of Thomas Hardy" and "The Crown." These expectations were at least partially disappointed. In *Sea and Sardinia* Lawrence reacted against the aspects of the island's primitivism that he had failed to anticipate. In the Indian dances and markets of *Mornings in Mexico* he found manifestations of the qualities of primitive life that he had been seeking, but he realized that he could not participate in them—not because of squeamishness, but for the more fundamental reason that as a modern European he was unable in an actual physical situation to put aside the mental-spiritual component of his own consciousness. The Etruscan places, however, provided only congenial suggestions which left ample opportunity for the free play of Lawrence's imagination. As I will demonstrate, *Etruscan Places* is concerned less with the analysis of a fully developed ancient civilization than with the projection of a possible future one.

One example of the integration of the narrative and analytical levels of the book is the portrait of the young German archaeology student who accompanies Lawrence and Brewster on their visit to the tombs of Tarquinia. He is as fully realized as any of the minor characters in Lawrence's fiction, but he also typifies the consciousness that is identified elsewhere in the book with the Romans, Mussolini, and modern science, while Lawrence himself represents the qualities that he identifies with the Etruscans. Furthermore, we see Lawrence in yet another role in *Etruscan Places*: that of a generalist commenting on the observations of specialized scholars, particularly Pericle Ducati and George Dennis, whose works he had studied in preparation for his excursion. In writing his essay on Volterra Lawrence even followed the organization of Dennis' chapter, giving, in the same order, observations on the city's geopraphy and history and on the appearance of the modern town and descriptions of such landmarks as the Porta all' Arco, the church of Santa Chiara, the monastery of San Giusto, and Le Balze—the huge cliffs that border the site of the Etruscan necropolis; Dennis, however, proceeds to the tombs, Lawrence to an account of a modern political gathering.[7] Characteristically, Lawrence used Dennis when he agreed with him and ignored him when he did not. Lawrence de-emphasized the evidence of the Etruscans' commercial and military activities that he found in Dennis' work and painted a picture of an essentially peaceful people who were on the whole humane and generous toward other tribes and nations and careful and sensitive in their stewardship of the land.[8] In any case, Lawrence's goal was not to popularize or emulate nineteenth-century scholarship but to give an account of the physical and imaginative worlds which he had himself experienced.

Etruscan Places shares with Lawrence's other travel books a focus on the contrast between the modern and primitive worlds, and between the modes of consciousness identified with each. As I have shown, *Twilight in Italy* describes the encroachment of the abstracted, impersonal Northern European way of life on rural Italy; *Sea and Sardinia* sets off primitive Sardinia against the relatively modernized mainland and against Lawrence's own modern prejudices, which he acknowledges with chagrin; *Mornings in Mexico* contrasts emotion-starved Americans who travel about the Southwest in automobiles with the New Mexican Indians whose ancient religious dances have become a tourist attraction. In *Etruscan Places* contemporary mechanicality and ennui confront primitive vitalism in the juxtaposition of the Italian present with the Etruscan past. As Ronald P. Draper writes of the second Tarquinia chapter, "Each time Lawrence and his friend Brewster descend into the Etruscan tombs, they enter a marvellous underground world which is not so much an escape from reality as the expression of a creative dissatisfaction with the devitalized world of the surface. Modern Italy and the Italy of its imagined past are counterpointed with poignant effect, and Lawrence himself moves in both worlds."[9] Lawrence's poignant sense of loss is highlighted in his descriptions of the contemporary appearance of the Etruscan sites. At Tarquinia, Lawrence recognizes in the "rather forlorn vacant lot" just inside the city gates what in Etruscan times must have been "a sacred clearing, with a little temple to keep it alert" (*EP*, 51; 25; 47). At Volterra, Lawrence and Brewster return to the town center after viewing a spectacular sunset in which it seems "as if the last hour had come, and the gods were smelting us all back into yellow transmuted oneness."

> But nothing is being transmuted. We turn our faces, a little frightened, from the vast blaze of gold, and in the dark, hard streets the town band is just chirping up, brassily out of tune as usual, and the populace, with some maidens in white, are streaming in crowds towards the piazza. And like the band, the populace is also out of tune, buzzing with the inevitable suppressed jeering. (*EP*, 181; 104; 169)

It is not only lost beauty Lawrence regrets, but lost wildness. He asks his guide at Vulci whether there is hunting in the hills nearby, and finds that the boar, the fox, and the deer are becoming more and more scarce. "Soon the only animals left will be tame ones: man the tamest and most swarming" (*EP*, 150; 86; 140). Lawrence finds only a forlorn hope that man is not fully tamed in the "full, dark, handsome jovial faces" of the women who crowd around the bus that serves Cerveteri (*EP*, 34-35; 16; 32-33), and in the "faun-face, not deadened by morals" of a shepherd he meets in a wine shop (*EP*, 15; 4; 14).

Yet the book's basic contrast is not between past and present so much as between the ancient Eastern mode of life represented by the Etruscans and the contrary mode embodied in the Greeks and Romans and the whole Western tradition that they began.[10] Lawrence writes that one feels for the Etruscans "instant sympathy, or instant contempt and indifference. Most people despise anything that isn't Greek, for the good reason that it ought to be Greek if it isn't. So Etruscan things are put down as a feeble Graeco-Roman imitation" (*EP*, 11-12; 1; 9-10). Lawrence's sympathy is clearly with the Etruscans, but while he criticizes the Graeco-Roman world-view, it is too important to the history of Western civilization to be regarded with indifference. He depicts ancient Rome, in particular, as a great negative force redolent of repression, militarism, and materialism. According to Lawrence the Romans suffered from what in an early version of *Lady Chatterley's Lover* Mellors calls the "one fatal disease" of Western civilization: "the lust of self-importance."[11] In contrast, Lawrence finds among Etruscan remains a sense of warmth and humanity.

> There is a queer stillness and a curious peaceful repose about the Etruscan places I have been to. . . . There is a stillness and a softness in these great grassy mounds with their ancient stone girdles, and down the central walk [at Cerveteri] there lingers still a kind of homeliness and happiness.
>
> (*EP*, 23; 9; 21)

He rejects the "uplift" of Greek and the "mass" of Roman monuments for the "ease, naturalness, and abundance of life" represented in Etruscan tombs, which show "no need to force the mind or soul in any direction" (*EP*, 28; 12; 26). According to Lawrence, the Etruscans lived and built on a natural scale, and their mode of living was attuned to the rhythms of nature; the conquering Romans sought to subjugate nature to human ends. Etruscan flowering gave way to Roman military force, the Etruscan culture declined into imitation, the Etruscan religion became superstition. Yet Lawrence sees the conflict as a continuing one, and one in which the Etruscan side will ultimately, in its quiet way, triumph:

> Yet the Etruscan *blood* continued to beat. And Giotto and the early sculptors seem to have been a flowering again of the Etruscan blood, always being trodden down again by some superior "force." It is a struggle between the endless patience of life and the endless triumph of force.
>
> (*EP*, 130; 75; 122)

In the same passage, Lawrence explains the opposition in terms of subjectivity and objectivity: the Etruscans had lived by a subjective control of nature, and "their subjective power fell before the objective power of the Romans." In *Etruscan Places*, rhetorically at least, the Etruscan consciousness, in the form of Lawrence's subjective, intuitive understanding of the Tarquinian tomb paintings, triumphs over the Roman-like objective knowledge of the young German archaeologist.

Lawrence's enlistment on the side of intuition as against objective scientific knowledge is hardly surprising, but the political dimension of his exposition of this polarity is important because it represents a significant alteration in his thinking since the early nineteen-twenties. David Cavitch has noted that in *Etruscan Places* Lawrence rejects his previous views on the drive for political power.[12] Lawrence insists that brute force is ultimately inferior, as a life principle, to sensitivity.

> Because a fool kills a nightingale with a stone, is he therefore greater than the nightingale? Because the Roman took the life out of the Etruscan, was he therefore greater than the Etruscan? Not he! Rome fell, and the Roman phenomenon with it. Italy to-day is far more Etruscan in its pulse than Roman: and always will be so. Why try to revert to the Latin-Roman mechanism and suppression? (*EP*, 57; 29; 53)

A casual reader of *The Plumed Serpent* might expect Lawrence to have approved of Mussolini, but throughout *Etruscan Places* Lawrence belittles fascism, which he sees as an attempt to revive the Roman imperium.[13] For example, Lawrence comments that Mussolini's restoration of the ancient name of Tarquinia to the town that had come to be known as Corneto is ironic, for in evoking the Etruscan past the fascist contradicts his self-identification as the rightful heir to Rome. For Lawrence the Etruscans were the least Roman of all Italian peoples, just as the Romans—and by extension the modern fascists—were the least Italian, the least attuned to the grace and ease of the native landscape (*EP*, 49; 24; 45). Lawrence's Etruscan tour seems to have strengthened his rejection, stated in the Epilogue to *Movements in European History*, of the inevitability of rule based on political and military force. Don Ramón in *The Plumed Serpent* is a transitional figure: he claims to derive his authority from a mystical connection with the cosmos, but he sometimes translates that authority into cruelty and repression. In *Etruscan Places* Lawrence maintains that the Etruscan oligarchs, the lucumones, similarly were religious seers who also functioned as temporal leaders, but that their ability to rule depended on the people's recognition of their greater natural sensitivity and wisdom rather than on force. "They were not aristocrats in the Germanic sense, nor even patricians in the Roman. They were first and foremost leaders in the sacred mysteries, then magistrates, then men of family and wealth" (*EP*, 59; 31; 55-56).[14] The nature of Lawrence's views concerning leadership and power in the years following his Etruscan tour is evidenced in a letter written to his young disciple Rolf Gardiner in 1928:

> I'm afraid the whole business of leaders and followers is somehow wrong, now. Like the demon-drive, even leadership must die, and be born different, later on. I'm afraid part of what ails you is that you are struggling to enforce an obsolete form of leadership... The reciprocity of power is obsolete. When you get down to the basis of life, to the depth of the warm

creative stir, there is no power. It is never: There *shall* be light!—only:
Let there be light! The same way, not: Thou *shalt* dance to the mother
earth!—only: Let it be danced to the mother earth![15]

Lawrence wrote in a similar vein to Witter Bynner that "the hero is obsolete,
and the leader of men a back number.... And the new relationship will be
some sort of tenderness, sensitive, between men and men and men and
women...."[16] Lawrence went on in this letter to reaffirm his commitment to
"the phallic reality, as against the non-phallic cerebration unrealities." The
goal is the same as Don Ramón's but the means—and the language—is that
of *Etruscan Places* and *Lady Chatterley's Lover*. Lawrence's sense of what
is important is now divorced from the idea of political power, and is centered in tenderness, the "warm creative stir" which he found embodied in
what he imagined to have been the Etruscan way of life. That these statements do not represent a revolution in Lawrence's thinking so much as a
reassertion of beliefs that had been obscured in his writing of the "leadership" novels can be demonstrated by considering the letter that he had written to Lady Ottoline Morrell in 1915 about his plan for a "Rananim" colony.

> The great serpent to destroy, is the will to Power: the desire for one man
> to have some dominion over his fellowmen. Let us have *no* personal in-
> fluence, if possible—nor personal magnetism, as they used to call it, nor
> persuasion—no 'Follow me'—but only 'Behold.' And a man shall not come
> [to Rananim] to save his own soul. Let his soul go to hell. He shall come
> because he knows that his own soul is not the be-all and the end-all, but
> that all souls of all things do but compose the body of God, and that God
> indeed shall *Be*.[17]

Although Lawrence had never totally abandoned this position, he despaired
during the later stages of the War and the years that followed of men ever
coming to such a realization on their own, and his despair led him to speculate about how spiritual renewal might be fostered by charismatic leaders
like Don Ramón Carrasco. The Etruscan example, however fanciful Lawrence's reconstruction of it may have been, seems to have rekindled his con-
fidence in the possibility of a coherent, creative society that would function
successfully without coercion from above.

In his account of Etruscan religion Lawrence again presents a contrast
between Etruscan naturalness and Graeco-Roman mental knowledge. The
late Etruscan paintings and artifacts from the 3rd Century B.C. onward reflect the conquered people's adoption of Hellenic polytheism, but the earlier
pieces are free from any representations of divinities. George Dennis refused
to accept the implications of this fact, and posited the theory that "in the

earlier ages of Etruria...the people were so enthralled by the hierarchy, that they may not have dared to represent, perhaps scarcely to contemplate, the mysteries of their creed...."[18] Lawrence, almost certainly extrapolating from his knowledge of the religion of the American Indians, asserts that the Etruscan religion was pre-theistic; it depended not on supplications to gods and goddesses but on a deep connection with the elemental powers of the physical universe. According to Lawrence the key symbol in early Etruscan religious art was the *patera*, which he saw represented in the tomb paintings of Tarquinia and the effigies at the Tarquinia museum.

> If it is a man, his body is exposed to just below the navel, and he holds in his hand the sacred *patera*, or *mundum*, the round saucer with the raised knob in the center, which represents the round germ of heaven and earth. It stands for the plasm, also, of the living cell, with its nucleus, which is the indivisible God of the beginning, and which remains alive and unbroken to the end, the eternal quick of all things, which yet divides and subdivides, so that it becomes the sun of the firmament and the lotus of the waters under the earth.... So within each man is the quick of him, when he is a baby, and when he is old, the same quick; some spark, some unborn and undying vivid life electron. (*EP*, 58; 29-30; 54)

For a people like the Etruscans who lived, as Lawrence put it later, "in naked contact with the cosmos, the whole cosmos...alive and in contact with the flesh of man,"[19] the idea of anthropomorphic gods and goddesses could not intrude, and the only possible symbol of divinity was an impersonal one like the *patera*. Lawrence speculates a great deal in the Tarquinia chapters about the significance of symbols like the *patera* and of scenes of augury he sees in the tomb paintings, but his purpose is not that of an antiquarian. In "The Etruscan Museum" he wrote:

> Civilizations rise in waves, and pass away in waves. And not till science, or art, tries to catch the ultimate meaning of the symbols that float on the last waves of the prehistoric period; that is, the period before our own; shall we be able to get ourselves into right relation with man as man is and has been and will always be.[20]

Lawrence considered an understanding and appreciation of the symbolic system of the Etruscans, as representatives of an earlier mode of consciousness, to be essential to the curve of return that he sought to follow.

The extent to which Lawrence's interpretations of the tomb paintings do catch the "ultimate meaning" of their symbols is doubtful, since they often reflect ideas which he had previously stated elsewhere. His discussion of the animals depicted on the walls of the tombs is reminiscent of the imagery of passages in *Twilight in Italy*, where the fundamental duality of the two infinites is expressed in terms of the Eagle and the Dove, the Tiger and the Lamb. In the Etruscan tombs we find "the continual repetition of lion against deer."

> As soon as the world was created, according to the ancient ideas, it took on duality. All things became dual, not only in the duality of sex, but in the polarity of action.... But [the animals] do not represent good action and evil action. On the contrary, they represent the polarised activity of the divine cosmos, in its animal creation. (*EP*, 99-100; 56; 93-94)

To the "mysterious conscious point of balance or equilibrium between the two halves of the duality" Lawrence now gives the name of "the soul," the "treasure of treasures...in every creature, in every tree or pool" (*EP*, 100; 56; 94). In *Twilight in Italy* he had called it the Holy Ghost; the change in terminology is significant, because it shifts the location of ultimate meaning from the realm of the abstract to that of the particular: Lawrence now makes clear his belief that the polarity exists, and has its dynamic reconciliation, first within the individual.

Lawrence repeatedly emphasizes the physicality of the Etruscan religion, calling attention to the stone phalluses and arxes (the house-shaped female symbols) that stand outside the tombs at Cerveteri. The convention in the Tarquinian tomb paintings of coloring men's bodies red is another symbol of the sacredness of the body. Here again Lawrence sees an analogy with the American Indians.

> The American Indian will tell you: "The red paint, it is medicine, make you see!" But he means medicine in a different sense from ours. It is deeper even than magic. Vermillion is the colour of his sacred or potent or god body. Apparently it was so in all the ancient world. Man all scarlet was his bodily godly self. (*EP*, 78; 42; 72)[21]

In the Etruscan figures Lawrence found an embodiment of the "blood-consciousness" that he had made a central element in his philosophy more than a dozen years before. This emphasis on the physicality of Etruscan religion is also evident in Lawrence's account of the Etruscan conception of death: "It was neither an ecstasy of bliss, a heaven, nor a purgatory of torment. It was just a natural continuance of the fulness of life. Everything was in terms of life, of living" (*EP*, 28; 12; 26). As a result Lawrence found it difficult and even pointless to speculate whether the tombs' many banquet scenes represented celebrations in this world or the next. It was because of the vitality of their representations that Lawrence failed to find the tombs (except the late, Romanized tombs of the Typhon and of Orcus) depressing in any sense.

86

One of the most enchanting of the painted tombs at Tarquinia is the Tomb of Hunting and Fishing, which is covered with small pictures of divers, fishermen bobbing about in little boats, and hunters aiming at flights of birds. The life represented there and in the other tombs was distinguished, for Lawrence, by its qualities of immediacy and spontaneity. The young German points out that a figure of a horse in one tomb has been redrawn, and Lawrence sees through the figure to a feeling of empathy with the ancient artist.

> He seems to have drawn the whole thing complete, each time, then changed the position, changed the direction, to please his feeling. And as there was no indiarubber to rub out the first attempts, there they are, from at least six hundred years before Christ: the delicate mistakes of an Etruscan who had the instinct of a pure artist in him, as well as the blithe insouciance which makes him leave his alterations for anyone to spy out, if they want to. (*EP*, 119-20; 67-68; 111-12)

The Tarquinian paintings are not realistic in technique, yet for Lawrence they captured "the natural flowering of life." In them Lawrence saw expressions of a "religion of life . . . a conception of the universe and man's place in the universe which made men live to the depth of their capacity" (*EP*, 88-89; 49; 83). This religion as Lawrence imagined it contained elements that resemble the animism of the American Indians.

> The whole thing [the cosmos] was live, and had a great soul, or *anima*: and in spite of one great soul, there were myriad roving, lesser souls: every man, every creature and tree and lake and mountain and stream, was animate, had its own peculiar consciousness. (*EP*, 89; 49; 83)

Here again Lawrence touches on the relationship of the individual to the whole. The whole, the universe, is alive, but its life is always manifested in particulars. The individual is part of the whole, but it is always supremely itself. And Lawrence understood even this wholeness in terms of a duality.

> The universe, which was a single aliveness with a single soul, instantly changed, the moment you thought of it, and became a dual creature with two souls, fiery and watery, for ever mingling and rushing apart, and held by the great aliveness of the universe in an ultimate equilibrium. But they rushed together and they rushed apart, and immediately they became myriad: volcanoes and seas, then streams and mountains, trees, creatures, men. (*EP*, 90; 49-50; 83-84)

This passage does much to explain the paradoxes that began to appear in Lawrence's writing as early as *Twilight in Italy*. The polarities of Father and Son, tiger and lamb, lion and deer—and, by implication, individual and community—are aspects of the one, the Holy Ghost, the soul, the living whole, as it is *apprehended by thought*. The wholeness can only be apprehended mystically or intuitively; rational thought (including Lawrence's own) immediately imposes divisions. Lawrence ascribes to the Etruscans his own tendency toward dialectical thinking, and, more importantly, a fundamental apprehension of a unity within and beyond diversity and duality.

It is in his descriptions of the Tarquinian tomb paintings that Lawrence expresses what he believes to have been the fundamental characteristic of Etruscan experience: the overriding importance of physical contact—of touch. What Lawrence means by "touch" is perhaps best explained in the course of his description of the Tomb of the Painted Vases:

> On one end wall is a gentle little banquet scene, the bearded man softly touching the woman with him under the chin. . . . Rather gentle and lovely is the way he touches the woman under the chin, with a delicate caress. That again is one of the charms of the Etruscan paintings: they really have the sense of touch; the people and the creatures are all really in touch. It is one of the rarest qualities, in life as well as in art. There is plenty of pawing and laying hold, but no real touch. In pictures especially, the people may be in contact, embracing or laying hands on one another. But there is no soft flow of touch. The touch does not come from the middle of the human being. It is merely a contact of surfaces and a juxtaposition of objects. . . . Here, in this faded Etruscan painting, there is a quiet flow of touch that unites the man and the woman on the couch, the timid boy behind, the dog that lifts his nose, even the very garlands that hang on the wall. (*EP*, 83-84; 45-46; 77-78)

Genuine touch and its importance to life stand at the thematic centre of the major works of Lawrence's final years. In the second version of *Lady Chatterley's Lover* Tommy Dukes, the most appealing of Clifford's cronies, theorizes, "There will be a civilization based on the mystery of touch, and all that that means; a field of consciousness which hasn't yet opened into existence. *We're* too afraid of it—oh, stiff as wood, with fear! We paw things—but probably we've never *truly* touched anybody in all our lives, nor any living thing. Oh, there'll be democracy—the democracy of touch."[22] What for Dukes is an impersonal speculation becomes for Mellors, in the novel's final version, a *credo*: "I stand for the touch of bodily awareness between human beings . . . and the touch of tenderness."[23] Genuine touch in the sense of the Etruscan paintings is seen, in Lawrence's late works, as the only way to overcome the isolation of the ego. In *The Escaped Cock* (first published as *The Man Who Died*), the resurrected Christ, after his first encounter with the priestess of Isis, ponders whether he is ready for the new life she offers: "Dare I come into touch? For this is further than death. I have dared to let them lay hands on me and put me to death. But dare I come into this tender touch of life?"[24] His physical consummation with the priestess transcends in its significance the spiritual consummation which he had achieved before the events of the novel began: "This is the great atonement, the being in touch."[25] Finally, the whole of Lawrence's *Last Poems*, his personal testament of death and resurrection, turns on the triumph of touch over idealism and mechanicality.

Being in touch meant for Lawrence not only personal connection with other individuals but a larger connection, which he believed the Etruscans had experienced, with the universe as a whole.

> It must have been a wonderful world, that old world where everything appeared alive and shining in the dusk of contact with all things, not merely as an isolated individual thing played upon by daylight; where each thing had a clear outline, visually, but in its very clarity was related emotionally or vitally to strange other things, one thing springing from another.... (*EP*, 120-21; 68; 112-13)

The word "wonderful" is not used carelessly here; Lawrence means the specific relation to experience that he had observed in the American Indians and that he later associated with his own response to the hymns of his childhood in the essay "Hymns in a Man's Life." Like the Indians, the Etruscans, according to Lawrence, preserved throughout their lives the capacity for wonder that is lost to men who habitually seek and depend upon objective knowledge.

> But it was by seeing all things alert in the throb of interrelated passional significance that the ancients kept the wonder and the delight in life, as well as the dread and the repugnance. They were like children: but they had the force, the power and the sensual *knowledge* of true adults. They had a world of valuable knowledge that is utterly lost to us.
> (*EP*, 122-23; 70; 114-15)

Throughout *Etruscan Places* Lawrence rejects the force, power, and knowledge represented by the Roman *imperium* and by modern mechanical civilization, but he affirms that true force, power, and knowledge—not for the sake of control but for the sake of life—are derived from and express themselves in the mystery of touch.

Etruscan Places thus contains not only Lawrence's expression of his understanding of a dead civilization, but also a guide for personal conduct in the present and a prescription for a more fulfilling society in an indefinite future. Edward Nehls has recognized the central importance of *Etruscan Places* to an understanding of Lawrence's later writing: "Having found in [the Etruscan past] the clue to living, he wrote his *Apocalypse* as a vision for which man might strive in the present."[26] Nehls errs, I believe, only in singling out *Apocalypse*; for the mystery of touch is shown in different ways to be the "clue to living" in virtually all of the works of Lawrence's final years. Although in and after *Etruscan Places* Lawrence de-emphasized the specifically political concerns that are reflected in *Kangaroo* and *The Plumed Serpent*, he never abandoned his concern for the future of mankind; most often, as in the following passage from *A Propos of* Lady Chatterley's Lover, his words reframe the lessons of the Etruscan tombs:

> Oh, what a catastrophe for man when he cut himself off from the rhythm of the year, from his unison with the sun and the earth. Oh, what a catastrophe, what a maiming of love when it was made a personal, merely personal feeling, taken away from the rising and the setting of the sun, and cut off from the magic connection of the solstice and the equinox! This is what is the matter with us, because we are cut off from the earth and sun and stars. . . .[27]

The late poem "Future Relationships" imagines a world in which politics are transfigured into a cosmic religion like that of the Etruscans, expressed not as "a democracy of idea or ideal, nor of property, nor even of the emotion of brotherhood. / But a democracy of men, a democracy of touch."[28] Community, in such a world, would be an expression of true selfhood: "Once men touch one another, then the modern industrial form of machine civilisation will melt away . . . the great movement of centralising into oneness will stop / and there will be a vivid recoil into separateness; / many vivid small states, like a kaleidoscope, all colours / and all the differences given expression."[29] Lawrence looks forward to a world in which men are sufficiently confident of their own identities, defined not by their power over one another but by their personal sense of being in touch with the cosmos and with other men and women, to refrain from forcing their wills on those around them and on the physical environment.

Somewhat surprisingly, England, not Italy or Mexico, became the primary focus for Lawrence's imaginative re-creation of a society based on the mystery of touch. In August 1926, during his final visit to his native country, Lawrence wrote to Earl Brewster, "Curiously, I like England again, now I am up in my own regions. It braces me up: and there seems a queer, odd sort of potentiality in the people, especially the common people. One feels in them some old, unaccustomed sort of plasm twinkling and nascent. They are not finished."[30] Lawrence's essay "Nottingham and the Mining Countryside," written in 1929 but most probably inspired by the memories of his childhood awakened during his 1925 and 1926 visits, expands upon the nature of this odd potentiality, describing the intimate underground community in which the miners worked and the sense of "naked contact" they brought with them when they returned home at evening; "and if I think of my childhood, it is always as if there was a lustrous sort of inner darkness, like the gloss of coal, in which we moved and had our real being."[31] It is no wonder that during Lawrence's visit to the Tarquinian tombs the dark world they embodied came to seem more real to him than the daylight world above (*EP*, 76; 40; 70). And "Nottingham and the Mining Countryside" presents Lawrence's native Eastwood as a sort of Etruria *manqué*:

> If the company, instead of building those sordid and hideous squares, then, when they had that lovely site to play with, there on the hill top: if they had put a tall column in the middle of the small marketplace, where people could stroll or sit, and with handsome houses behind. . . . If above all, they had encouraged song and dancing. . . . If only they had done this, there would never have been an industrial problem. The industrial problem arises from the base forcing of all human energy into a competition of mere acquisition.[32]

For Lawrence the drive for acquisition is a manifestation, on the lowest level, of the desire to give expression to the individual ego. The sordidness of modern industrial society is a result of its failure to foster the development of the intrinsic, primal self. "Nottingham and the Mining Countryside" ends with Lawrence's answer to what he sees as the deadness of contemporary England: tear it down, village by village, and in each community build handsome homes around a vital civic centre; in other words, remake it in the Etruscan mold. A similar sense of England's potential for rebirth is suggested in *Lady Chatterley's Lover* when Mellors describes his formula for bringing about a regeneration of the English working classes:

> "If you could only tell them that living and spending isn't the same thing. . . . If the men wore scarlet trousers as I said, they wouldn't think so much of money: if they could dance and hop and skip, and sing and swagger and be handsome, they could do with very little cash. And amuse the women themselves, and be amused by the women. They ought to learn to be naked and handsome, and to sing in a mass and dance the old group dances, and carve the stools they sit on, and embroider their own emblems. Then they wouldn't need money."[33]

In *A Propos of* Lady Chatterley's Lover, Lawrence explicitly connects these ideas to the goal of phallic knowledge and the emphasis on touch that pervades *Etruscan Places*: "If England is to be regenerated . . . then it will be by the arising of a new blood-contact, a new touch, and a new marriage."[34] The answer to the "industrial problem" that Lawrence offers through Mellors sounds like little more than the adoption of the mode of living of an idealized Middle Ages, or perhaps some kind of revival of Ruskin's Guild of St. George; it conveniently sweeps away modern demographic realities and ignores the tenacity of existing political and economic institutions. Yet in the abstract Mellors' enumeration of the preconditions for such a society rings true: "clean up the country again. An' not have many children, because the world is overcrowded."[35] In a world even more cosmopolitan, more economically centralized, and more dependent upon technology than Lawrence's, Mellors' voice is beginning to be heard again, not only through organizations like Friends of the Earth and Zero Population Growth but in the form of calls for decentralization and the development of "appropriate" (often small-scale) technologies by the late economist E. F. Schuhmacher and the advocacy of "soft energy paths" by the British physicist Amory Lovins.[36]

Mellors' tone is rather wistful ("If only you could . . ."), and even to Lawrence the chance for the rebirth of England as an island of small, self-sufficient communities whose members find meaning through crafts, singing, and dancing must have seemed remote. Yet in these same years some of Lawrence's ideas were actually being put into practice on a small scale by a young man named Rolf Gardiner; and Lawrence, in turn, was undoubtedly influenced by Gardiner's work.[37] Lawrence had been Gardiner's culture-hero since Gardiner had read *Twilight in Italy*, and the two corresponded throughout the nineteen-twenties. Gardiner helped to arrange a series of exchanges between English and German youth groups in the years after World War I. He founded the English Travelling Morrice and went about England in search of traditional dances and songs. In 1927 he acquired a farm in Dorset where he established the community of Springhead on a plan of economic, cultural, and religious restoration. Springhead was thus a kind of practical realization of Lawrence's earlier vague dreams of the utopian community of Rananim. Lawrence was enthusiastic and encouraging. Soon after the founding of Springhead he wrote to Gardiner:

> The English must have kindled again for them their religious sense of at-one-ness. And for that you must have a silent, central flame, a flame of *consciousness* and of warmth which radiates out bit by bit. Keep the core sound, and the rest will look after itself. What we need is reconciliation and atoning. I utterly agree with your song, dance and labour; but the core of atoning in the few must be there, if your song, dance and labour are to be a real source.[38]

What Lawrence meant by "the core of atoning" is obscure, but it *is* clear that he conceived of social renewal as beginning with spiritual renewal within the individual, a passionate commitment of a religious nature. Lawrence's letters to Gardiner suggest that for a time, especially before Springhead became a reality, he considered joining the experiment, and he offered suggestions about practical arrangements. But an early letter demonstrates that his reluctance to commit himself to *any* movement—even one in which he would presumably have occupied a special position—would have finally prevented him from taking part.

> I should love to be connected with something, with some few people, in something. As far as anything *matters*, I have always been very much alone, and regretted it. But I can't belong to clubs, or societies, or Freemasons, or any other damn thing. So if there is, with you, an activity I *can* belong to, I shall thank my stars. But, of course, I shall be wary beyond words, of committing myself.[39]

It should be remembered that Lawrence's entire mature life was characterized by rootlessness. After he left Eastwood he was never in any real sense a member of a community, and the only place he seems to have thought of as a "home" was Kiowa Ranch, where he lived for a total of less than twelve months. While he returned again and again to the *idea* of belonging to a community, in practice Lawrence carefully guarded his independence.

Nevertheless, his knowledge of Gardiner's experiment almost certainly nourished Lawrence's vision of the regeneration of England and its expression in *A Propos of* Lady Chatterley's Lover, where he insisted on the necessity of getting "back into relation, vivid and nourishing relation to the cosmos and the universe. The way is through daily ritual, and the re-awakening. ... To these rituals we must return; or we must evolve them to suit our needs. ... We must plant ourselves again in the universe."[40] There are echoes here of the ritualism of *The Plumed Serpent*, but the background of civil strife and military force has been replaced by the overtone of tenderness established in *Lady Chatterley's Lover* and a sense of potential which grew out of Gardiner's founding on English soil of an actual community based on Lawrentian principles.

All of this may seem somewhat distant from *Etruscan Places*, but the connection is made clear when one considers Lawrence's autobiographical fantasy, first published in *Phoenix* but apparently written in October 1927.[41] The fantasy describes Lawrence falling asleep in the countryside near Nottingham and awakening a thousand years later to find a civilization of natural, fulfilled men and women living a life of meaningful labor and ritual in a beautiful town that has been erected on the hill of Eastwood. Keith Sagar has recognized that the natives of the imagined community display the "physical awareness and intimate togetherness" of Lawrence's Etruscans.[42] Lawrence's imagined scene of the Etruscans returning at evening to Tarquinia is almost directly paralleled in the autobiographical fantasy.

93

And surely, in those days, young nobles would come spashing in on horseback, riding with naked limbs on an almost naked horse, carrying probably a spear, and cantering ostentatiously through the throng of red-brown, full-limbed, smooth-skinned peasants. (*EP*, 106; 59; 98)

Three horsemen came cantering up, from behind. All the world was turning home towards the town, at sunset. The horsemen slackened pace as they came abreast. They were men in soft, yellow sleeveless tunics with the same still, formal Egyptian faces and trimmed beards as my companions. Their arms and legs were bare, and they rode without stirrups. . . . There was a great stillness in all the world, and yet a magic of close-interwoven life.[43]

The vision in the fantasy is of a reborn Eastwood of the thirtieth century, a community of whole, self-integrated men and women, "body and mind and spirit, without split," living in organic unity. Here as among Lawrence's Etruscans, the basis of life is the naturally ordered movement of ritual dance as an expression of the mystery of touch. Such a community, based not on force but on a sense of wonder derived from the contact between the individual and the universe, would presumably resolve the conflict between communal purpose and individual freedom that had troubled Lawrence since the "Study of Thomas Hardy" and before. In *Studies in Classic American Literature* Lawrence wrote, "Men are free when they are obeying some deep, inward voice of religious belief. Obeying from within. Men are free when they belong to a living, organic, *believing* community, active in fulfilling some unfulfilled, perhaps unrealized purpose."[44] This is the kind of community that Lawrence believed existed among the Etruscans and that he envisions in the autobiographical fantasy: a community that depends upon and fosters true selfhood instead of generating self-conscious striving and economic competition. The fantasy ends with the injunction of a man in a red tunic, an English *lucumone* of the thirtieth century: "Why are you afraid to be a butterfly that wakes up out of the dark for a little while, beautiful? Be beautiful, then, like a white butterfly. Take off your clothes and let the firelight fall on you. What is given, accept then—"[45]

And *Etruscan Places*, too, is ultimately a book of acceptance—but not of Lawrence's world as it was, or of the imagined life of a dead culture, or of the inevitability of death. Rather, it is a book of acceptance of the continual challenge of life. David Cavitch has observed that as he neared death "The current of Lawrence's imagination turned entirely inward, and his significant artistic achievements in his last years arose from an almost saintly contemplation of his own dying."[46] Yet even then Lawrence's mind retained the restlessness that had always characterized it. *Lady Chatterley's Lover* ends not with a marriage but with the possibility of a new kind of marriage; the resurrected Christ of *The Escaped Cock* does not come to rest at the temple of Isis but continues his journey; *Last Poems* concludes with the stirring of new life in the ashes of the phoenix. In the closing pages of *Apocalypse* Lawrence could still write of his sense of the need for community, a community in which the self would be in organic harmony with the whole. In 1927 he wrote to Trigant Burrow of the danger of suppression of the societal instinct.

> What ails me is the absolute frustration of my primeval societal instinct. The hero illusion starts with the individualist illusion, and all resistances ensue. I think societal instinct is much deeper than sex instinct—and societal repression much more devastating. There is no repression of the sexual individual comparable to the repression of the societal man in me, by the individual ego, my own and everybody else's.[47]

Lawrence's choice of words is significant: in *Last Poems* the "ego" is the "fallen self," the modern, mechanical, illusory self that must be consigned to oblivion before the true self can be reborn, free to participate in true communal experience. As his resistance to direct involvement in Gardiner's Springhead project indicates, Lawrence was never able to put aside his individual ego sufficiently to take practical steps toward the fulfillment of his "societal instinct." In spite of his continued insistence that for his fulfillment a man must realize that he is a "collective being," he was describing himself when he wrote of modern man, "*We cannot bear connection.* That is our malady. We *must* break away, and be isolate."[48] Lawrence had recognized, by his final years, that true community required a personal intensity of which his contemporaries, who in Ezra Pound's words had accepted "the press for wafer; / Franchise for circumcision," were incapable. And he too, in spite of his convictions, was unable to overcome his felt need for isolation. The eloquent and often-quoted passage with which he concluded *Apocalypse* demonstrates his belief that the remaking of society depends on the remaking of the self. Lawrence maintains that "individualism is ... an illusion," but his mystical injunction to "start with the sun" indicates a paradoxical belief that social regeneration must be founded on individual reawakenings.

> What we want is to destroy our false, inorganic connections, especially those related to money, and re-establish the living organic connections, with the cosmos, the sun and earth, with mankind and nation and family. Start with the sun, and the rest will slowly, slowly happen.[49]

In *Etruscan Places* Lawrence's impulse of mind, his desire to construct a coherent plan of living, and his impulse of world, his need to depict life as he saw it, are at last integrated. But mind and world could become one only

95

because the "world" of that book existed primarily in Lawrence's imagination; the Etruscans were not present to qualify and perhaps contradict his conception of them. Yet the accuracy or inaccuracy of Lawrence's account of the Etruscans is finally unimportant. *Etruscan Places* is not a book of history or of cultural anthropology. It records Lawrence's visit to the remains of a lost civilization, and it builds on those remains to establish the vision of human potential that informs all of Lawrence's last works, a vision of creative community based on direct experience: the mystery of touch.

The book's closing passage symbolizes the gentleness of that vision, which is one of the triumph of creativity over the will to power and one that affirms the importance of individual humanity within an organic society. Lawrence describes the fortress of Volterra, now a prison, and retells some anecdotes about it.

> There were also two men who escaped. Silently and secretly they carved likenesses of themselves out of the huge loaves of hard bread the prisoners get. Hair and all, they made their own effigies lifelike. Then they laid them in the bed, so that when the warder's light flashed on them he should say to himself: "There they lie sleeping, the dogs!"
> And so they worked, and they got away. It cost the governor, who loved his house of malefactors, his job. He was kicked out. It is curious. He should have been rewarded for having such clever children, sculptors in bread. (*EP*, 198-99; 115; 186-87)

The prisoners defy authority, not through violence but through art, to gain their freedom—much as in the art of his travel books Lawrence charted a path from the prison of the modern mechanized world back through dead and dying civilizations to a point from which new possibilities for freedom and fulfillment could be seen shining in the untravelled distances. Lawrence's travel books demonstrate that the pattern underlying his life and work was one of continual growth and opening of consciousness. It has often been observed that Lawrence's books *end*, but never *conclude*; this characteristic of his style reflects the belief in openness to experience that is perhaps best expressed in a passage from the unpublished final chapter of *Etruscan Places*.

> Man is always trying to be conscious of the cosmos, the cosmos of life and passion and feeling, as well as of physical phenomena. And there are still millions of undreamed-of ways of becoming aware of the cosmos. Which is to say, there are millions of worlds, whole cosmic worlds, to us yet unborn.[50]

In his own life Lawrence never resolved the tension between his defiant individualism and his longing for community, but in *Etruscan Places* he showed how he believed that division might be overcome by others. The value of Lawrence's final vision lies in its suggestion that if people could, by following the example of their primitive ancestors, become more sensitive to each other and to their environment, a world in which the individual need not be at odds with his community might be possible. The potential for human fulfillment that Lawrence saw in the mystery of touch was projected on the distant future, a future that could never be realized by external political effort but only by the individual—and eventually collective—awakenings of generations of men and women who had followed the curve of return.

NOTES

CHAPTER I

[1] See Lawrence's Preface to his *Collected Poems* (1928) in *The Complete Poems of D. H. Lawrence*, ed. Vivian de Sola Pinto and F. Warren Roberts, 3rd ed. (New York: Viking, 1971), p. 27.

[2] David Cavitch, *D. H. Lawrence and the New World* (New York: Oxford Univ. Press, 1969), p. 107.

[3] D. H. Lawrence, *Aaron's Rod* (1922; New York: Viking Compass, 1971), p. 98.

[4] Baruch Hochman, *Another Ego: The Changing View of Self and Society in the Work of D. H. Lawrence* (Columbia, S.C.: Univ. of South Carolina Press, 1970), p. 261.

[5] Earl and Achsah Brewster, *D. H. Lawrence: Reminiscences and Correspondence* (London: Martin Secker, 1934), p. 166.

[6] D. H. Lawrence, *Studies in Classic American Literature* (1923); New York: Viking Compass, 1961), pp. 5-6. Cf. D. H. Lawrence, *The Symbolic Meaning: The Uncollected Versions* of Studies in Classic American Literature, ed. Armin Arnold (New York: Viking, 1964), p. 20, and D. H. Lawrence, *Psychoanalysis and the Unconscious* and *Fantasia of the Unconscious* (1921, 1922; New York: Viking Compass, 1960), p. 165.

[7] Billy T. Tracy, "D. H. Lawrence and the Travel Book Tradition," *D. H. Lawrence Review*, 11 (Fall, 1978), 285-86.

[8] John Alcorn, *The Nature Novel from Hardy to Lawrence* (New York: Columbia Univ. Press, 1977), p. x.

[9] Alcorn, p. 58.

[10] Alcorn, p. 50.

[11] S. Ronald Weiner, "The Rhetoric of Travel: The Example of *Sea and Sardinia*," *D. H. Lawrence Review*, 2 (Fall, 1969), 231.

[12] Edward Nehls, "D. H. Lawrence and the Spirit of Place," in *The Achievement of D. H. Lawrence*, ed. Frederick J. Hoffman and Harry T. Moore (Norman, Okla.: Univ. of Oklahoma Press, 1953), p. 269.

[13] Letter to Lady Ottoline Morrell (1 February 1915), *The Collected Letters of D. H. Lawrence*, 2 vols., ed. Harry T. Moore (London: Heinemann, 1962), I, 311.

[14] George J. Zytaryuk, ed., *The Quest for Rananim: D. H. Lawrence's Letters to S. S. Koteliansky 1914 to 1930* (Montreal and London: McGill-Queens Univ. Press, 1970), pp. 62-63.

[15] Zytaryuk, pp. 71-72.

[16] See Harry T. Moore, *The Priest of Love: A Life of D. H. Lawrence* (New York: Farrar, Straus and Giroux, 1974), p. 362.

[17] Knud Merrild, *With D. H. Lawrence in New Mexico: A Memoir of D. H. Lawrence* (New York: Barnes and Noble, 1965), p. 251.

[18] D. H. Lawrence, *Phoenix: The Posthumous Papers of D. H. Lawrence,* ed. Edward P. McDonald (London: Heinemann, 1936), p. 343.

[19] D. H. Lawrence, *Women in Love* (1920; New York: Viking Compass, 1960), p. 308. See Alcorn, pp. 96-97.

[20] D. H. Lawrence, "On Being Religious," *Phoenix,* pp. 729-30.

[21] Emile Delavenay, *D. H. Lawrence: The Man and His Work. The Formative Years: 1885-1919,* trans. Katharine M. Delavenay (Carbondale and Edwardsville, Ill.: Southern Illinois Univ. Press, 1972), p. xvi.

[22] *Phoenix,* p. 447. That Lawrence continued to make this distinction throughout his career is demonstrated in "The Florence Museum," the unpublished seventh chapter of *Etruscan Places.* The MS is in the possession of the Humanities Research Center at the University of Texas, Austin. Lawrence wrote, "These are two separate things: the artistic or impulsive or culture-expression, and the religious or scientific or civilization expression, of a group of people. The first is based on emotion; the second on concepts" (p. 5).

[23] Letter to Ernest Collings (17 January 1913), *Collected Letters,* I, 180.

[24] Reprinted in R. P. Draper, ed., *D. H. Lawrence: The Critical Heritage* (New York: Barnes and Noble, 1970), p. 163.

[25] Moore, *Priest of Love,* p. 62.

[26] Aldous Huxley, "Introduction," *The Letters of D. H. Lawrence* (New York: Viking, 1932), p. xxx.

[27] See Chapter XIII, "Mino," *Women in Love.*

[28] *Complete Poems,* p. 490.

[29] Moore, *Priest of Love,* pp. 26-27, 29-31, 40.

[30] Moore, *Priest of Love,* pp. 54-55.

[31] *Phoenix,* p. 411.

[32] Stephen J. Miko, in *Toward Women in Love: The Emergence of a Lawrentian Aesthetic* (New Haven and London: Yale Univ. Press, 1971), p. 189, recognizes manifestations of this tendency in the closing chapters of *The Rainbow* and the opening chapters of "Study of Thomas Hardy."

[33] D. H. Lawrence, *Phoenix II: Uncollected, Unpublished and Other Prose*

Works, ed. Warren Roberts and Harry T. Moore (London: Heinemann, 1968), p. 567.

[34] F. von Broembsen, "Mythic Identification and Spatial Inscendence: The Cosmic Vision of D. H. Lawrence," *Western Humanities Review*, 29 (Spring, 1975), 153.

[35] Alcorn, p. 119.

[36] Broembsen, pp. 142-143.

[37] *Studies in Classic American Literature*, pp. 136-37.

CHAPTER II

[1] The final chapters, "Italians in Exile" and "The Return Journey," however, were written after Lawrence's walking tour south over the Alps in September, 1913.

[2] Rose Marie Burwell, "A Catalogue of D. H. Lawrence's Reading from Early Childhood," *D. H. Lawrence Review*, 3 (Fall, 1970), 202.

[3] Burwell, 203, 206, 207, 210. Though Lawrence's use of the concept of "Self" and "Not-Self" in *Twilight in Italy* seems to be related to Hegel's, there is no conclusive evidence of the extent of Lawrence's familiarity with Hegel's works. Similarly, while there are many echoes in Lawrence of Schopenhauer's antithesis between reason and insight and between theoretical and immediate knowledge, Schopenhauer cannot confidently be cited as a direct source for the dualistic ideas expressed in *Twilight in Italy*. For a discussion of the likely influence on Lawrence of Nietzsche's *The Birth of Tragedy*, see James C. Cowan, "D. H. Lawrence's Dualism: The Apollonian-Dionysian Polarity and *The Ladybird*," in *Forms of Modern British Fiction*, ed. Alan Warren Friedman (Austin, Texas: Univ. of Texas Press, 1975), pp. 73-78.

[4] Letter to Rolf Gardiner (3 December 1926), *Collected Letters*, II, 952.

[5] D. H. Lawrence, "Nottingham and the Mining Countryside," *Phoenix*, p. 135.

[6] "Nottingham and the Mining Countryside," *Phoenix*, p. 136.

[7] Delavenay, p. 186. H. M. Daleski in *The Forked Flame: A Study of D. H. Lawrence* (London: Faber and Faber, 1965) sees Lawrence's philosophizing as an integral part of his creative process.

[8] Delavenay, p. 186.

[9] *Complete Poems*, pp. 182-83.

[10] Letter to Ernest Collings (17 January 1913), *Collected Letters*, I, 180.

[11] Richard Aldington, "Introduction," *Twilight in Italy* by D. H. Lawrence, Phoenix Edition (London: Heinemann, 1956), p. ix. See also Aldington, *Portrait of a Genius, But* ... (London: Jonathan Cape, 1954), p. 93;

"Italian Sketches," *Times Literary Supplement* (15 June 1916), 284; and Delavenay, p. 337.

[12] Mark Schorer, "Introduction," *Poste Restante: A D. H. Lawrence Travel Calendar* by Harry T. Moore (Berkeley and Los Angeles: Univ. of California Press, 1956), pp. 10-11.

[13] Delavenay, p. 342.

[14] *Collected Letters*, I, 364.

[15] D. H. Lawrence, "Italian Studies: By the Lago di Garda," *The English Review*, 15 (September, 1913), 231.

[16] Letter to Ernest Collings (17 January 1913), *Collected Letters*, I, 179. See also *Collected Letters*, I, 150 and 203-4.

[17] Aldous Huxley, "Introduction," *Letters*, p. xxvii.

[18] Nehls, p. 275.

[19] Nehls, p. 272.

[20] William A. Fahey, "Lawrence's San Gaudenzio Revisited," *D. H. Lawrence Review*, 1 (Spring, 1968), 51.

[21] Nehls, p. 271.

[22] Delavenay, p. 341.

[23] Hochman, p. 85.

[24] *Phoenix II*, pp. 365-67.

[25] Eugene Goodheart, *The Utopian Vision of D. H. Lawrence* (Chicago: Univ. of Chicago Press, 1963), p. 95.

[26] *Phoenix II*, pp. 373-74.

[27] Miko, p. 293.

[28] Jessie Chambers [E.T.], *D. H. Lawrence: A Personal Record* (1935), new ed., edited by J. D. Chambers (New York: Barnes and Noble, 1965), pp. 104-05.

[29] *Phoenix II*, p. 223.

[30] "Study of Thomas Hardy," *Phoenix*, p. 475.

[31] *Phoenix II*, p. 412.

CHAPTER III

[1] Anthony Burgess, "Introduction," *D. H. Lawrence and Italy* (New York: Viking Compass, 1972), p. xii.

[2] Keith Aldritt, *The Visual Imagination of D. H. Lawrence* (Evanston, Ill.: Northwestern Univ. Press, 1971), p. 226.

[3] Aldritt, p. 226.

[4] See Moore, *Poste Restante*, pp. 61-62.

⁵ In a letter to J. C. Squire dated March 7, 1921 (*Collected Letters*, II, 645), Lawrence indicated that he was "just finishing" the book; Lawrence was correcting the manuscript by March 16 (*Collected Letters*, II, 646), and on April 4 he sent it to his agent, Curtis Brown (*Collected Letters*, II, 647).

⁶ David Ellis, "Reading Lawrence: The Case of *Sea and Sardinia*," *D. H. Lawrence Review*, 10 (Spring, 1977), 53.

⁷ Nicholas Joost and Alvin Sullivan, *D. H. Lawrence and "The Dial"* (Carbondale, Ill.: Southern Illinois Univ. Press, 1970), pp. 58-59.

⁸ Letter to Curtis Brown (4 April 1921), *Collected Letters*, II. 647.

⁹ *Collected Letters*, II, 678. Lawrence's phrase seems just. *The Dial* published, in October, 1921, three paragraphs from pp. 4-5 of Lawrence's typescript (now in the Lawrence collection at the Humanities Research Center, Univ. of Texas at Austin) and a longish section from pp. 6-11 under the title "As Far as Palermo." In the typescript that chapter is 29 pages long. "The Sea" received similar treatment. In November the chapters "Cagliari," "To Mandas," "To Sorgono," and "To Nuoro" were represented by brief excerpts. As edited, *The Dial*'s "Sea and Sardinia" has no narrative continuity and reads like a loosely related group of impressionistic sketches.

¹⁰ Henry B. Fuller, "Sardinian Days," *The Freeman*, 4 (1 March 1922), 595.

¹¹ Cavitch, p. 118. See also Francis Hackett, "A Week in D. H. Lawrence," *The New Republic*, 29 (11 January 1922), 184; and Richard Mayne, "*Sea and Sardinia* Revisited," *New Statesman and Nation*, 59 (18 June 1960), 899.

¹² Richard Aldington, "Introduction," *Sea and Sardinia* by D. H. Lawrence, Phoenix Edition (London: Heinemann, 1956), p. ix.

¹³ Cavitch, p. 115.

¹⁴ Mayne, 899. See also Carl Van Doren's review in *The Nation*, 114 (4 January 1922), 19.

¹⁵ Cavitch, p. 117.

¹⁶ *Phoenix*, pp. 446-47.

¹⁷ *Psychoanalysis and the Unconscious* and *Fantasia of the Unconscious*, pp. 134-35.

¹⁸ Letter to Bertrand Russell (26 February 1915), *Collected Letters*, I, 323-24.

¹⁹ Cavitch, p. 117.

²⁰ Nehls, p. 279.

²¹ D. H. Lawrence, *Kangaroo* (1923; rpt. New York: Viking Compass, 1961), p. 216.

[22] Weiner, 235.

[23] Weiner, 235-36.

[24] Philip Rieff, "Introduction," *Psychoanalysis and the Unconscious* and *Fantasia of the Unconscious*, p. xv.

[25] *Psychoanalysis and the Unconscious* and *Fantasia of the Unconscious*, p. 60.

[26] *Psychoanalysis and the Unconscious* and *Fantasia of the Unconscious*, pp. 132-33.

[27] See Chapter I, above.

[28] *The Dial*, 72 (February, 1922), 196.

[29] D. H. Lawrence, *Sea and Sardinia*, typescript, Humanities Research Center, Univ. of Texas, p. 139.

[30] Letter to Rosalind Popham (2 March 1921), *Collected Letters*, II, 644.

CHAPTER IV

[1] D. H. Lawrence, "New Mexico," *Phoenix*, p. 142.

[2] *Phoenix*, p. 144.

[3] Letter to Earl Brewster (16 November 1921), *Collected Letters*, II, 677.

[4] *Collected Letters*, II, 715.

[5] Letter to Earl Brewster (22 September 1922), *Collected Letters*, II, 717.

[6] Richard Aldington, "Introduction" to *Mornings in Mexico*, in *Mornings in Mexico and Etruscan Places*, Phoenix Edition (London: Heinemann, 1956), p. vi.

[7] L. D. Clark, *The Dark Night of the Body: D. H. Lawrence's* The Plumed Serpent (Austin, Texas: Univ. of Texas Press, 1964), p. 48.

[8] F. Warren Roberts, *Bibliography of D. H. Lawrence* (London: Rupert Hart-Davis, 1963), pp. 83-84. There are no significant differences between the texts of the articles and that of *Mornings in Mexico*. Indeed, there are few alterations from the manuscripts.

[9] London: John Murray, 1903.

[10] "New Mexico," *Phoenix*, pp. 146-47.

[11] Dexter Martin, "D. H. Lawrence and Pueblo Religion: An Inquiry into Accuracy," *Arizona Quarterly*, 9 (1953), 222, 232.

[12] See, for example, "Poetry of the Present," *Complete Poems*, pp. 181-86.

[13] William York Tindall, *D. H. Lawrence and Susan His Cow* (New York: Columbia Univ. Press, 1939), pp. 107-09.

[14] Frederick Carter, *The Dragon of the Alchemists* (London: Elkin Matthews, 1926). See *Collected Letters*, II, 744, and Edward McDonald's Introduction to *Phoenix*, pp. xviii-xix.

[15] *Psychoanalysis and the Unconscious* and *Fantasia of the Unconscious*, p. 55.

[16] Cambridge, Mass.: The Peabody Museum, 1901, p. 479.

[17] Philadelphia: David McKay, 1843.

[18] D. H. Lawrence, "The Hopi Snake Dance," holograph manuscript, Humanities Research Center, Univ. of Texas at Austin, p. 6.

[19] Frederick Carter, *The Dragon of Revelation* (London: Desmond Harmsworth, 1931), pp. 65-66. Lawrence's interest in these ideas is confirmed in Carter's account of a visit from Lawrence in January, 1924, in his book *D. H. Lawrence and the Body Mystical* (London: Dennis Archer, 1932), pp. 34-35. Another possible source of the dragon images in *MM* is in Lewis Spence's *The God's of Mexico* (New York: Frederick A. Stokes, 1923), p. 18, where Spence points out that in Mexican myth "the earth is represented as a monster known as *cipactli*, whose pictorial representations resemble a dragon, "the earth-monster common to the mythologies of many races. . . ."

[20] Letter to Willard Johnson (? August 1924), *Collected Letters*, II, 802-04.

[21] *Phoenix II*, pp. 324-25.

[22] *Studies in Classic American Literature*, p. 136.

[23] Ronald P. Draper, *D. H. Lawrence* (London: Twayne, 1964), p. 26.

[24] *Phoenix*, p. 99.

[25] Thomas R. Whitaker, "Lawrence's Western Path: 'Mornings in Mexico,'" *Criticism*, 3 (Summer, 1961), 219-36.

[26] The idea is probably a simplification of Spence's account of the Aztec belief in *The Gods of Mexico*, pp. 37-39.

[27] Whitaker, 223.

[28] Whitaker, 225.

[29] Although it was completed and published in 1920, *The Lost Girl* was "three parts done" before the War. Letter to Martin Secker (27 December 1919), *Collected Letters*, I, 602.

[30] Hochman, p. 168.

[31] Scott Sanders, *D. H. Lawrence: The World of the Five Major Novels* (New York: Viking, 1974), p. 152.

[32] D. H. Lawrence, "Education of the People," *Phoenix*, p. 608. The essay was written in 1920.

[33] See, for example, "Aristocracy" (1925), *Phoenix II*, pp. 477, 483-84.

[34] Burwell, 204, 210, 212.

[35] Thomas Carlyle, *Past and Present* (1843; rpt. London: Chapman and Hall, 1895), p. 189.

[36] Frederick William Roe, *The Social Philosophy of Carlyle and Ruskin* (1921; rpt. New York: The Gordian Press, 1970), pp. 88-89.

[37] Thomas Carlyle, *Heroes and Hero Worship* (1841; rpt. London: Chapman and Hall, 1895), p. 182.

[38] John Ruskin, *The Works of John Ruskin,* ed. E. T. Cook and Alexander Wedderburn, 39 vols. (London: George Allen, 1903-1912), XVII, 111.

[39] Roe, pp. 271-87.

[40] *Collected Letters*, II, 859.

[41] D. H. Lawrence, *The Plumed Serpent* (New York: Alfred A. Knopf, 1926), p. 190. See also pp. 245, 358-60.

[42] Cavitch, pp. 187-88.

[43] Sanders, p. 166.

[44] Mark Schorer, *The World We Imagine* (New York: Farrar, Straus and Giroux, 1948), p. 128.

[45] Clark, p. 83.

[46] *Complete Poems*, p. 339.

[47] *Phoenix*, p. 714.

[48] Quoted in Roe, p. 207.

[49] *Phoenix*, p. 715.

[50] *Phoenix*, p. 761.

[51] *Phoenix*, pp. 761-62.

[52] Letter to Curtis Brown (30 September 1924), *Collected Letters*, II, 810.

[53] D. H. Lawrence, *Movements in European History* (1921), new ed., edited by James Boulton (London: Oxford Univ. Press, 1971), p. 317.

[54] *Movements in European History*, p. 318.

[55] *The Plumed Serpent*, p. 271.

[56] *The Plumed Serpent*, p. 177.

[57] *Phoenix*, p. 31.

[58] Daleski, pp. 223-24.

[59] *Women in Love*, p. 72.

[60] Letter to Else Jaffe (27 September 1922), *Collected Letters*, II, 720.

[61] *Studies in Classic American Literature*, pp. 137-38.

[62] *Studies in Classic American Literature*, pp. 136-37.

[63] D. H. Lawrence, "[*The Dragon of the Apocalypse*, by Frederick Carter]," *Phoenix*, p. 301.

[64] D. H. Lawrence, "Certain Indians and an Englishman" (1922), *Phoenix II*, p. 243.

[65] Letter to Rolf Gardiner (4 July 1924), *Collected Letters*, II, 796. Cf. the letter to Lady Ottoline Morrell (1 February 1915), *Collected Letters*, I, 311, quoted in Chapter I.

[66] "Democracy," *Phoenix*, p. 713.

[67] James C. Cowan, *D. H. Lawrence's American Journey: A Study in Literature and Myth* (Cleveland: The Press of Case Western Reserve Univ., 1970), p. 141.

CHAPTER V

[1] Letter to John Middleton Murry (4 January 1926), *Collected Letters*, II, 876.

[2] Letter to Catherine Carswell (25 October 1921), *Collected Letters*, II, 668.

[3] Letter to Curtis Brown (5 April 1926), *Collected Letters*, II, 895.

[4] Letter to Earl Brewster (9 June 1927), *Collected Letters*, II, 984.

[5] Letter to Alfred A. Knopf (10 October 1927), *Collected Letters*, II, 1108.

[6] Christopher Hassall, "Black Flowers: A New Light on the Poetics of D. H. Lawrence," *A D. H. Lawrence Miscellany*, ed. Harry T. Moore (Carbondale, Ill.: Southern Illinois Univ. Press, 1959), p. 370.

[7] Cf. George Dennis, *The Cities and Cemeteries of Etruria* (London: John Murray, 1883), II, 136-47, and D. H. Lawrence, *Etruscan Places* (London: Martin Secker, 1932), pp. 173-80. For an extended discussion of Lawrence's use of Dennis, see Billy T. Tracy, "'Reading up the Ancient Etruscans': Lawrence's debt to George Dennis," *Twentieth Century Literature*, 23 (December, 1977), 437-50.

[8] Tom Morris, "On Etruscan Places," *Paunch*, 40-41 (1975), 19-20.

[9] Draper, p. 27.

[10] Morris discusses the contrast in *EP* between the Etruscan and Roman modes of life at length.

[11] D. H. Lawrence, *John Thomas and Lady Jane* (New York: Viking Compass, 1974), p. 99.

[12] Cavitch, p. 209.

[13] Morris points out that everything in Italian Fascist doctrine but the ideas of power and leadership "is in radical opposition to Lawrence's own view of a better social order as suggested by *Etruscan Places*" (Morris, 30). As I shall demonstrate, even Lawrence's views on leadership and power differed considerably from those of the Fascists.

[14] Tracy points out that Lawrence accepted George Dennis' interpretation of the Etruscan social structure, but did not share Dennis' distaste for the Etruscans' oligarchic system or his belief that its basis was wealth. Law-

rence chose to see the *lucumones* as examples of the "natural aristocrats" he had described in the essay "Aristocracy" Tracy, "'Reading up the Ancient Etruscans,'" 445-47.

[15] Letter to Rolf Gardiner (4 March 1928), *Letters*, pp. 712-13.

[16] Letter to Witter Bynner (13 March 1928), *Collected Letters*, II, 1045.

[17] Letter to Lady Ottoline Morrell (1 February 1915), *Collected Letters*, I, 312.

[18] Dennis, I, 382.

[19] D. H. Lawrence, *Apocalypse* (1931; New York: Viking Compass, 1966), p. 160.

[20] D. H. Lawrence, "The Florence Museum," *Etruscan Places*, holograph manuscript, Humanities Research Center, Univ. of Texas at Austin, p. 5.

[21] Cf. "For the Heroes are Dipped in Scarlet," *Complete Poems*, p. 688.

[22] *John Thomas and Lady Jane*, p. 58.

[23] D. H. Lawrence, *Lady Chatterley's Lover* (New York: Grove Press, 1962), p. 348.

[24] D. H. Lawrence, *The Escaped Cock*, ed. Gerald M. Lacy (Los Angeles: Black Sparrow Press, 1973), p. 46.

[25] *The Escaped Cock*, p. 58.

[26] Nehls, p. 285.

[27] *Phoenix II*, p. 508.

[28] *Collected Poems*, p. 611.

[29] "Future States," *Collected Poems*, p. 611.

[30] Letter to Earl Brewster (30 August 1926), *Collected Letters*, II, 933.

[31] *Phoenix*, pp. 135-36.

[32] *Phoenix*, p. 138.

[33] *Lady Chatterley's Lover*, p. 372. Cf. "Red Trousers" (1928), *Phoenix II*, pp. 562-64.

[34] *Phoenix II*, p. 508.

[35] *Lady Chatterley's Lover*, p. 281.

[36] E. F. Schuhmacher, *Small is Beautiful* (New York: Harper and Row, 1973); Amory Lovins, *Soft Energy Paths* (Cambridge, Mass.: Ballinger, 1977).

[37] See W. J. Keith, "Spirit of Place and *Genius Loci*: D. H. Lawrence and Rolf Gardiner," *D. H. Lawrence Review*, 7 (Summer, 1974), 127-38.

[38] Letter to Rolf Gardiner (7 January 1928), *Letters*, p. 706.

[39] Letter to Rolf Gardiner (?22 July 1926), *Collected Letters*, II, 928.

[40] *Phoenix II*, p. 510.

[41] D. H. Lawrence, "[Autobiographical Fragment]," *Phoenix*, pp. 817-36. The piece is incomplete and untitled in manuscript. Edward McDonald's provisional title is somewhat misleading, since only the opening pages are autobiographical in the factual sense. A more accurate and evocative title appears on the folder in which the manuscript is kept in the Bancroft Library at the University of California at Berkeley: "Newthorpe in 2927." The date of composition is implied by a reference on p. 835 of *Phoenix*.

[42] Keith Sagar, *The Art of D. H. Lawrence* (Cambridge: Cambridge Univ. Press, 1966), p. 314.

[43] *Phoenix*, pp. 829-30.

[44] *Studies in Classic American Literature*, p. 6.

[45] *Phoenix*, p. 836.

[46] Cavitch, p. 205.

[47] Letter to Trigant Burrow (13 July 1927), *Collected Letters*, II, 989-90.

[48] *Apocalypse*, p. 198.

[49] *Apocalypse*, p. 200.

[50] "The Florence Museum," p. 3.

BIBLIOGRAPHY

I. Published Works by D. H. Lawrence

Aaron's Rod. 1922; rpt. New York: Viking Compass, 1961.

"Ancient Metropolis of the Etruscans." *Travel*, 50 (December, 1927), 20-25, 50.

Apocalypse. 1931; rpt. New York: Viking Compass, 1966.

"As Far as Palermo." *The Dial*, 71. (October, 1921), 441-51.

"Cagliari." *The Dial*, 71. (November, 1921), 583-92.

"City of the Dead at Cerveteri." *Travel*, 50 (November, 1927), 12-16, 50.

The Collected Letters of D. H. Lawrence. Ed. Harry T. Moore. 2 vols. London: Heinemann, 1962.

The Complete Poems of D. H. Lawrence. Ed. Vivian de Sola Pinto and F. Warren Roberts. 3rd ed. New York: Viking Compass, 1971.

The Complete Short Stories of D. H. Lawrence. 3 vols. New York: Viking Compass, 1961.

"The Dance of the Sprouting Corn." *Theatre Arts Monthly*, 8 (July, 1924), 447-57.

The Escaped Cock. 1929; new ed., edited by Gerald M. Lacy. Santa Barbara, Cal.: Black Sparrow, 1973.

Etruscan Places. London: Martin Secker, and New York: Viking, 1932.

Etruscan Places [with *Mornings in Mexico*]. Introduction by Richard Aldington. Phoenix Edition. London: Heinemann, 1956.

Etruscan Places. New York: Viking Compass, 1957.

"The Gentle Art of Marketing in Mexico." *Travel*, 46 (April, 1926), 7-9, 44.

"The Hopi Snake Dance." *Theatre Arts Monthly*, 8 (December, 1924), 836-860.

"Indians and Entertainment." *New York Times Magazine* (26 October 1924), pp. 3, 11.

"Italian Studies: By the Lago di Garda." *The English Review*, 15 (September, 1913), 202-34.

John Thomas and Lady Jane. New York: Viking Compass, 1974.

Kangaroo. 1923; rpt. New York: Viking Compass, 1961.

Lady Chatterley's Lover. 1928; rpt. New York: Grove Press, 1962.

"A Little Moonshine with Lemon." *Laughing Horse*, no. 13 (April, 1926), pp. 1-15.

The Letters of D. H. Lawrence. Ed. with an Introduction by Aldous Huxley. New York: Viking, 1932.

The Lost Girl. 1921; rpt. New York: Viking Compass, 1968.

Mornings in Mexico. London: Martin Secker, 1927.

Mornings in Mexico [with *Etruscan Places*]. Introduction by Richard Aldington. Phoenix Edition. London: Heinemann, 1956.

"Mornings in Mexico: Corasmin and the Parrots." *Adelphi*, 3 (December, 1925), 480-89, 502-06.

"Mornings in Mexico: The Mozo." *Adelphi*, 4 (February, 1927), 474-87.

"Mornings in Mexico: Walk to Huyapa." *Adelphi*, 4 (March, 1927), 538-554.

Movements in European History. 1921; new ed., edited by James Boulton. London: Oxford Univ. Press, 1971.

"The Painted Tombs of Tarquinia." *Travel*, 50 (January, 1928), 28-33, 40.

Phoenix: The Posthumous Papers of D. H. Lawrence. Ed. Edward D. McDonald. London: Heinemann, 1936.

Phoenix II: Uncollected, Unpublished and Other Prose Works. Ed. Warren Roberts and Harry T. Moore. London: Heinemann, 1968.

The Plumed Serpent. 1926; New York: Alfred A. Knopf, 1959.

Pscyhoanalysis of the Unconscious and *Fantasia of the Unconscious.* 1921, 1922; new edition, with an Introduction by Philip Rieff. New York: Viking Compass, 1960.

The Quest for Rananim: D. H. Lawrence's Letters to S. S. Koteliansky 1914 to 1930. Ed. George P. Zytaryuk. Montreal and London: McGill-Queens Univ. Press, 1970.

The Rainbow. 1915; rpt. New York: Viking Compass, 1961.

Sea and Sardinia. New York: Thomas Seltzer, 1921.

Sea and Sardinia. Introduction by Richard Aldington. Phoenix Edition. London: Heinemann, 1956, corrected 1964.

Sea and Sardinia. Introduction by Richard Aldington. New York: Viking Compass, 1963.

"Sea and Sardinia: As Far as Palermo; The Sea." *The Dial*, 71 (October, 1921), 441-51.

"Sea and Sardinia: Cagliari; To Mandas; Sorgono: The Inn; To Nuoro." *The Dial*, 71 (November, 1921), 583-92.

Sons and Lovers. 1913; rpt. New York: Viking Compass, 1958.

"Spirit of Place." *The English Review*, 27 (November, 1918), 319-31.

St. Mawr and *The Man Who Died*. 1925, 1931; rpt. New York: Vintage, 1953.

Studies in Classic American Literature. 1923; rpt. New York: Viking Compass, 1964.

"Sunday Stroll in Sleepy Mexico." *Travel*, 48 (November, 1926), 30-35, 60.

The Symbolic Meaning: The Uncollected Versions of Studies in Classic American Literature. Ed. Armin Arnold. New York: Viking, 1964.

Twilight in Italy. London: Duckworth, 1916.

Twilight in Italy. Introduction by Richard Aldington. Phoenix Edition. London: Heinemann, 1956.

Twilight in Italy. New York: Viking Compass, 1962.

"The Windswept Strongholds of Volterra." *Travel*, 50 (February, 1928), 31-35, 44.

Women in Love. 1920; rpt. New York: Viking Compass, 1960.

II.   Manuscripts of Works by D. H. Lawrence

"Autobiographical Fragment." Holograph manuscript (Bancroft Library, Univ. of California at Berkeley).

Etruscan Places

1. Autograph manuscript (Humanities Research Center, Univ. of Texas at Austin).
2. Typescript (Texas)
3. Type copy of "The Painted Tombs of Tarquinia" and "Vulci" (Texas).
4. Typescript of "The Painted Tombs of Tarquinia" and "Vulci" (Texas).
5. Notes for *Etruscan Places* (Berkeley).

Mornings in Mexico

1. "Friday Morning." Autograph manuscript (Texas).
2. "Friday Morning [deleted]," typescript (Texas).
3. "Sunday Morning," autograph manuscript (Texas).
4. "Monday Morning," autograph manuscript (Texas).
5. "Monday Morning," composite typescript and type copy (Texas).
6. "Saturday Morning," autograph manuscript (Texas).
7. "Indians and Entertainment," holograph manuscript (Berkeley).
8. "Indians and Entertainment," typescript (Berkeley).

111

9. "The Hopi Snake Dance," autograph manuscript (Texas).
10. "A Little Moonshine with Lemon," typescript and type copy (Texas).
11. "A Little Moonshine with Lemon," type copy [variant version] (Texas).

Sea and Sardinia
1. Type copy (Texas).

Twilight in Italy
1. "Christs in the Tirol," autograph manuscript (Texas).
2. "Christs in the Tirol," type copy (Texas).

III. Works by Other Authors

Aiken, Conrad. "Mr. Lawrence's Prose" [review of *MM*]. *The Dial*, 83 (October, 1927), 343-46.

Alcorn, John. *The Nature Novel from Hardy to Lawrence.* New York: Columbia Univ. Press, 1977.

Aldington, Richard. *Portrait of a Genius, But . . . : The Life of D. H. Lawrence, 1855-1930.* London: Heinemann, 1950.

Aldritt, Keith. *The Visual Imagination of D. H. Lawrence.* Evanston, Ill.: Northwestern Univ. Press, 1971.

Arnold, Armin. *D. H. Lawrence and America.* London: Linden Press, 1958.

Ball, Arthur. "Lawrence in Etruria" [review of *EP*]. *Bookman* (London), 83 (October, 1932), 49.

Bandelier, Adolph. *The Delight Makers.* New York: Dodd, Mead, 1918.

———. *The Gilded Man.* New York: D. Appleton, 1893.

Beals, Carlton. "Acknowledge the Wonder" [review of *MM*]. *The Nation*, 125 (14 September, 1927), 257-58.

Bedient, Calvin. *Architects of the Self.* Berkeley: Univ. of California Press, 1972.

Beker, Miroslav. "'The Crown,' 'The Reality of Peace,' and *Women in Love*." *D. H. Lawrence Review*, 2 (Fall, 1969), 254-64.

Benedict, Ruth. *Patterns of Culture.* Boston: Houghton Mifflin, 1934.

Blavatsky, H. P. *The Secret Doctrine.* 3 vols. London: Theosophical Publishing House, 1893.

Brett, Dorothy. *Lawrence and Brett: A Friendship.* Philadelphia: J. B. Lippincott, 1933.

Brewster, Earl and Achsah. *D. H. Lawrence: Reminiscences and Correspondence.* London: Martin Secker, 1934.

Broembsen, F. von. "Mythic Identification and Spatial Inscendence: The Cosmic Vision of D. H. Lawrence." *Western Humanities Review*, 29 (Spring, 1975), 137-54.

Brotherston, J. G. "Revolution and the Ancient Literature of Mexico, for D. H. Lawrence and Antonin Artaud." *Twentieth Century Literature*, 18 (July, 1972), 181-89.

Burgess, Anthony. "Introduction." *D. H. Lawrence and Italy*. New York: Viking Compass, 1972.

Burwell, Rose Marie. "A Catalogue of D. H. Lawrence's Reading from Early Childhood." *DHLR*, 3 (Fall, 1970), 193-324.

Bynner, Witter. *Journey with Genius: Recollections and Reflections Concerning D. H. Lawrence*. New York: Octagon Books, 1974.

————. "A Person with a Pen" [review of *MM*]. *New Republic*, 52 (12 October, 1927), 216-17.

Carlyle, Thomas. *Heroes and Hero Worship*. London: Chapman and Hall, 1895.

————. *Past and Present*. London: Chapman and Hall, 1895.

Carswell, Catherine. *The Savage Pilgrimage: A Narrative of D. H. Lawrence*. London: Martin Secker, 1932.

Carter, Frederick. *D. H. Lawrence and the Body Mystical*. London: Denis Archer, 1932.

————. *The Dragon of the Alchemists*. London: Elkin Matthews, 1926.

————. *The Dragon of Revelation*. London: Desmond Harmsworth, 1931.

Cavitch, David. *D. H. Lawrence and the New World*. New York: Oxford Univ. Press, 1969.

Chambers, Jesse ("E.T."). *D. H. Lawrence: A Personal Record* (1935). 2nd edition, ed. J. D. Chambers. New York: Barnes and Noble, 1965.

Clark. L. D. "D. H. Lawrence and the American Indian." *DHLR*, 9 (Fall, 1976), 305-72.

————. *Dark Night of the Body: D. H. Lawrence's* The Plumed Serpent. Austin, Texas: Univ. of Texas Press, 1964.

"A Colorful Portrait of a Picturesque Region" [review of *SS*]. *Boston Evening Transcript* (21 January 1922), 4: 9.

Colum, Padraic. "Sea and Sardinia" [review]. *The Dial*, 72 (February, 1922), 193-96.

Cowan, James C. *D. H. Lawrence's American Journey: A Study in Literature and Myth*. Cleveland: The Press of Case Western Reserve Univ., 1970.

————. "D. H. Lawrence's Dualism: The Apollonian-Dionysian Polarity and *The Ladybird*." *Forms of Modern Brititsh Fiction*. Ed. Alan Warren Friedman. Austin, Texas: Univ. of Texas Press, 1975.

Cyriax, Tony. *Among Italian Peasants*. New York: E. P. Dutton, 1919.

"D. H. Lawrence" [review of *The Prussian Officer* and *TI*]. *The Nation*, 104 (15 March 1917), 313-14.

Daleski, H. M. *The Forked Flame: A Study of D. H. Lawrence*. London: Faber and Faber, 1965.

Delavenay, Emile. *D. H. Lawrence and Edward Carpenter*. New York: Taplinger, 1971.

——. *D. H. Lawrence: The Man and His Work. The Formative Years: 1885-1919*. Transl. Katharine M. Delavenay. Carbondale and Edwardsville, Ill.: Southern Illinois Univ. Press, 1972.

Dennis, George. *The Cities and Cemeteries of Etruria*. 2 vols. London: John Murray, 1883.

Diaz, Bernal. *The True History of the Conquest of New Spain*. Transl. Alfred Percival Maudslay. 5 vols. London: Hakluyt Society, 1908-1916.

Draper, Ronald P. *D. H. Lawrence*. London: Twayne, 1964.

——. *D. H. Lawrence: The Critical Heritage*. New York: Barnes and Noble, 1970.

Eisenstein, Samuel A. *Boarding the Ship of Death: D. H. Lawrence's Quester Heroes*. The Hague and Paris: Mouton, 1974.

Ellis, David. "Reading Lawrence: The Case of *Sea and Sardinia*." *DHLR*, 10 (Spring, 1977), 52-63.

"Etruscan Places" [review]. *The Nation*, 136 (1 February 1933), 128.

"Etruscan Places" [review]. *Times Literary Supplement* (23 February 1933), p. 122.

Fahey, William A. "D. H. Lawrence's San Gaudenzio Revisited." *DHLR*, 1 (Spring, 1968), 51-56.

Fay, Eliot. *Lorenzo in Search of the Sun: D. H. Lawrence in Italy, Mexico, and the American South-West*. London: Vision Press, 1955.

Foster, Joseph. *D. H. Lawrence in Taos*. Albuquerque, N.M.: Univ. of New Mexico Press, 1972.

Fuller, Henry B. "Sardinian Days" [review of *SS*]. *The Freeman*, 4 (1 March 1922), 595-6.

Gersh, Gabriel. "In Search of D. H. Lawrence's *Sea and Sardinia*." *Queen's Quarterly*, 80 (Winter, 1973), 581-88.

Goodheart, Eugene. *The Utopian Vision of D. H. Lawrence*. Chicago: Univ. of Chicago Press, 1963.

Gordon, David J. *D. H. Lawrence as a Literary Critic*. New Haven and London: Yale Univ. Press, 1966.

Gransden, K. W. "Rananim: D. H. Lawrence's Letters to S. S. Koteliansky." *Twentieth Century*, 159 (January, 1956), 22-32.

Gregory, Horace. *D. H. Lawrence: Pilgrim of the Apocalypse.* 1933; rpt. Freeport, N.Y.: Books for Libraries Press, 1970.

———. "D. H. Lawrence: The Phoenix and the Grave." *New Republic*, 73 (14 December 1932), 131-33.

Gunn, Drewey Wayne. *American and British Writers in Mexico, 1556-1973.* Austin, Tex. and London: Univ. of Texas Press, 1974.

Gutierrez, Donald. "D. H. Lawrence's Golden Age." *DHLR*, 9 (Fall, 1976), 377-408.

Gutierrez de Lara, L., and Edgcumb Pinchon. *The Mexican People: Their Struggle for Freedom.* Garden City, N.Y.: Doubleday, Page, 1914.

Hackett, Francis. "A Week in D. H. Lawrence" [review of *SS*]. *New Republic*, 29 (11 January 1922), 184-85.

Harrison, Jane Ellen. *Ancient Art and Ritual.* New York: Holt and London: Williams and Norgate, 1913.

Hassall, Christopher. "Black Flowers: A New Light on the Poetics of D. H. Lawrence." *A D. H. Lawrence Miscellany*, ed. Harry T. Moore. Carbondale, Ill.: Southern Illinois Univ. Press, 1959, pp. 370-77.

———. "D. H. Lawrence and the Etruscans." *Essays by Divers Hands*, 31 (1962), 61-78.

Hochman, Baruch. *Another Ego: The Changing View of Self and Society in the Work of D. H. Lawrence.* Columbia, S.C.: Univ. of South Carolina Press, 1970.

Hough, Graham. *The Dark Sun: A Study of D. H. Lawrence.* New York: Macmillan, 1957.

Howe, Marguerite Beede. *The Art of the Self in D. H. Lawrence.* Athens, Ohio: Ohio Univ. Press, 1977.

Hutchinson, Percy. "D. H. Lawrence Delves in the Deep Past" [review of *EP*]. *New York Times Book Review* (11 December 1932), p. 4.

Huxley, Aldous. "Lawrence in Etruria" [review of *EP*]. *The Spectator*, 149 (4 November 1932), 629.

Inniss, Kenneth. *D. H. Lawrence's Bestiary: A Study of His Use of Animal Trope and Symbol.* The Hague and Paris: Mouton, 1971.

"Italian Sketches" [review of *TI*]. *Times Literary Supplement* (15 June 1916), p. 284.

Jarrett-Kerr, Martin. *D. H. Lawrence and Human Existence.* 1951; rpt. London: SCM Press, 1961.

Joost, Nicholas. *Scofield Thayer and* The Dial. Carbondale, Ill.: Southern Illinois Univ. Press, 1964.

Joost, Nicholas, and Alvin Sullivan. *D. H. Lawrence and* The Dial. Carbondale, Ill.: Southern Illinois Univ. Press, 1970.

Keith, W. J. "Spirit of Place and *Genius Loci*: D. H. Lawrence and Rolf Gardiner." *DHLR*, 7 (Summer, 1974), 127-38.

Kermode, Frank. *D. H. Lawrence*. New York: Viking, 1973.

Lane, James W. "Etruscan Places" [review]. *Bookman* (New York), 76 (January, 1933), 77-78.

"Lawrence Among the Etruscans" [review of *EP*]. *New Statesman and Nation*, 4 (22 October 1932), 490-92.

Lawrence, Frieda. *"Not I, But the Wind...."* New York: Viking, 1934.

Leavis, F. R. *D. H. Lawrence: Novelist*. New York: Alfred A. Knopf, 1956.

————. *Thought, Words and Creativity: Art and Thought in D. H. Lawrence*. New York: Oxford Univ. Press, 1976.

Lovins, Amory, *Soft Energy Paths*. Cambridge, Mass.: Ballinger, 1977.

Luhan, Mabel Dodge. *Lorenzo in Taos*. New York: Alfred A. Knopf, 1932.

Martin, Dexter. "D. H. Lawrence and Pueblo Religion: An Inquiry into Accuracy." *Arizona Quarterly*, 9 (1953), 219-34.

Mayne, Richard. *"Sea and Sardinia* Revisited." *New Statesman and Nation*, 59 (18 June 1960), 899-900.

Merrild, Knud. *With D. H. Lawrence in New Mexico: A Memoir of D. H. Lawrence*. New York: Barnes and Noble, 1965.

Miko, Stephen J. *Toward* Women in Love: *The Emergence of a Lawrentian Aesthetic*. New Haven and London: Yale Univ. Press, 1971.

Mitchell, Peter Todd. "Lawrence's *Sea and Sardinia* Revisited." *Texas Quarterly*, 8 (Spring, 1965), 67-72.

Mommsen, Theodor. *The History of Rome*. Transl. Rev. William P. Dickson. 4 vols. London: Bentley, 1862.

"Moods and Phantasies" [review of *MM*]. *Saturday Review*, 144 (20 August 1927), 281.

Moore, Harry T. *Poste Restante: A Lawrence Travel Calendar*. Introduction by Mark Schorer. Berkeley and Los Angeles: Univ. of California Press, 1956.

————. *The Priest of Love: A Life of D. H. Lawrence*. New York: Farrar, Straus and Giroux, 1974.

"Mornings in Mexico" [review]. *The Independent*, 119 (15 October 1927), 389.

"Mornings in Mexico" [review]. *TLS* (7 July 1927), p. 468.

Morrill, Claire. "Taos Echoes of D. H. Lawrence." *Southwest Review*, 47 (Spring, 1962), 150-56.

Morris, Tom. "On *Etruscan Places*." *Paunch*, 40-41 (1975), 8-39.

Moynahan, Julian. *The Deed of Life: The Novels and Tales of D. H. Lawrence*. Princeton: Princeton Univ. Press, 1963.

"Mr. Lawrence Presents the Mexicans" [review of *MM*]. *New York Times Book Review* (7 August 1927), p. 2.

"Mr. Lawrence's Spiritual Home" [review of *SS*]. *The Nation and the Athenaeum*, 33 (12 May 1923), 197.

Murry, J. Middleton. *D. H. Lawrence: Son of Woman*. 1931; rpt. London: Jonathan Cape, 1954.

Nahal, Chaman. *D. H. Lawrence: An Eastern View*. London: Thomas Yoseloff, 1970.

Nehls, Edward. *D. H. Lawrence: A Composite Bibliography*. 3 vols. Madison, Wis.: Univ. of Wisconsin Press, 1959.

————. "D. H. Lawrence: The Spirit of Place." *The Achievement of D. H. Lawrence*. Ed. Frederick J. Hoffmann and Harry T. Moore. Norman, Okla.: Univ. of Oklahoma Press, 1953, pp. 268-90.

"Never-Never Lands" [review of *EP*]. *Saturday Review*, 154 (12 November 1932), 509.

Nichols, Ann Eljenholm. "Syntax and Style: Ambiguities in Lawrence's *Twilight in Italy*." *College Composition and Communication*, 16 (December, 1965), 261-66.

Nin, Anais. *D. H. Lawrence: An Unprofessional Study*. 1932; rpt. Denver: Alan Swallow, 1964.

Nulle, Stebleton H. "D. H. Lawrence and the Fascist Movement." *New Mexico Quarterly*, 10 (February, 1940), 3-15.

Nuttall, Zelia. *The Fundamental Principles of Old and New World Religions*. Cambridge, Mass.: The Peabody Museum, 1901.

Oppenheim, E. C. "Lawrence and Etruria" [review of *EP*]. *The Spectator*, 149 (23 December 1932), 893.

Ossendowski, Ferdinand Antoni. *Beasts, Men and Gods*. New York: E. P. Dutton, 1922.

Panichas, George A. *Adventure in Consciousness: The Meaning of D. H. Lawrence's Religious Quest*. The Hague and Paris: Mouton, 1964.

Plowman, Max. "*Etruscan Places* and *Apocalypse*" [review]. *Adelphi*, n.s. 5 (February, 1933), 383-85.

Prescott, W. H. *History of the Conquest of Mexico*. 3 vols. Philadelphia: David McKay, 1843.

Pritchard, R. E. *D. H. Lawrence: Body of Darkness*. Pittsburgh: Univ. of Pittsburgh Press, 1971.

Pruette, Lorine. "With the Etruscans Lawrence Found Peace" [review of *EP*]. *New York Herald Tribune Books* (13 November 1932), p. 5.

Quennel, Peter. "Mr. Lawrence in Mexico" [review of *MM*]. *New States-man*, 26 (23 July 1927), 481-82.

Roberts, F. Warren. *Bibliography of D. H. Lawrence*. The Soho Bibliographies. London: Rupert Hart-Davis, 1963.

Roe, Frederick William. *The Social Philosophy of Carlyle and Ruskin*. 1921; rpt. New York: The Gordian Press, 1970.

Ruskin, John. *The Works of John Ruskin*. Ed. E. T. Cook and Alexander Wedderburn. 39 vols. London: George Allen, 1903-1912.

Sagar, Keith. *The Art of D. H. Lawrence*. Cambridge: Cambridge Univ. Press, 1966.

Sanders, Scott. *D. H. Lawrence: The World of the Five Major Novels*. New York: Viking, 1974.

Schaffner, Halle. "Lawrence Broods in the Sun" [review of *MM*]. *The Survey*, 59 (1 November 1927), 166-67.

Schorer, Mark. *The World We Imagine*. New York: Farrar, Straus and Giroux, 1948.

Schuhmacher, E. F. *Small is Beautiful*. New York: Harper and Row, 1973.

"Sea and Sardinia" [review]. *The American Review of Reviews*, 65 (February, 1922), 224.

Spence, Lewis. *The Gods of Mexico*. New York: Frederick A. Stokes, 1923.

Spender, Stephen, ed. *D. H. Lawrence: Novelist, Poet, Prophet*. New York: Harper and Row, 1973.

Spilka, Mark. *The Love Ethic of D. H. Lawrence*. Bloomington, Ind.: Indiana Univ. Press, 1955.

Swan, Michael. "Lawrence the Traveller." *London Magazine*, 4 (June, 1957), 46-51.

Taggard, Genevieve. "The Little Ghost in D. H. Lawrence" [review of *MM*}. *New York Herald Tribune Books* (7 August 1927), p. 5.

Tedlock, E. W., Jr. *D. H. Lawrence: Artist and Rebel*. Albuquerque, N.M.: Univ. of New Mexico Press, 1963.

Tenenbaum, Louis "Two Views of the Modern Italian: D. H. Lawrence and Sean O'Faolain." *Italica*, 37 (June, 1960), 118-25.

Tillyard, E. M. W. *Some Mythical Elements in English Literature*. London: Chatto and Windus, 1961.

Tindall, William York. *D. H. Lawrence and Susan His Cow*. New York: Columbia Univ. Press, 1939.

Tomlinson, H. M. *Gifts of Fortune*. London: Heinemann, 1927.

Tracy, Billy T. "D. H. Lawrence and the Travel Book Tradition." *DHLR*, 11 (Fall, 1978), 272-93.

———. "'Reading up the Ancient Etruscans': Lawrence's Debt to George Dennis." *Twentieth Century Literature*, 23 (December, 1977), 437-50.

"Travel and Travellers" [review of *MM*]. *The Nation and Athenaeum*, 41 (13 August 1927), 642.

Tylor, Edward B. *Primitive Culture*. 2 vols. London: John Murray, 1903.

Van Doren, Carl. "Sea and Sardinia" [review]. *The Nation*, 114 (4 January 1922), 19.

Vickery, John B. "The Plumed Serpent and the Reviving God." *Journal of Modern Literature*, 2 (November, 1972), 505-32.

Vivante, Leone. *A Philosophy of Potentiality*. London: Routledge and Kegan Paul, 1955.

Vivas, Eliseo. *D. H. Lawrence: The Failure and The Triumph of Art*. Evanston, Ill.: Northwestern Univ. Press, 1960.

Walsh, Thomas. "*Mornings in Mexico*" [review]. *The Commonweal*, 6 (28 September 1927), 504-05.

Weege, Fritz. *Etruskische Malerei*. Halle: Max Niemeyer, 1921.

Weiner, S. Ronald. "The Rhetoric of Travel: The Example of *Sea and Sardinia*." *DHLR*, 2 (Fall, 1969), 230-44.

Widmer, Kingsley. *The Art of Perversity: D. H. Lawrence's Shorter Fiction*. Seattle: Univ. of Washington Press, 1962.

Whitaker, Thomas R. "Lawrence's Western Path: *Mornings in Mexico*." *Criticism*, 3 (Summer, 1961), 219-36.

Wilkinson, Clennell. "Mornings in Mexico" [review]. *The London Mercury*, 27 (December, 1927), 218-19.

———. "Sea and Sardinia" [review]. *The London Mercury*, 8 (October, 1923), 667.

Williams, Raymond. "The Social Thinking of D. H. Lawrence." *A D. H. Lawrence Miscellany*, ed. Harry T. Moore. Carbondale, Ill.: Southern Illinois Univ. Press, 1959, pp. 295-311.

www.ingramcontent.com/pod-product-compliance
Lightning Source LLC
Chambersburg PA
CBHW061832040426
42447CB00012B/2928